The Art of Parables

Praise for The Art of Parables

Charles McCollough's art captures the drama, humour, and irony of Jesus' parables in a way that no prose interpretation can. Jesus used parables to trouble the waters of the known world and assail its easy assumptions. In McCollough's art, ancient waters tremble once again.
~ STEPHEN J. PATTERSON, AUTHOR OF *BEYOND THE PASSION: RETHINKING THE DEATH AND LIFE OF JESUS*

Charles McCollough's sculptures give us a new and arresting way of seeing Jesus' parables. In addition, his text provides us with the historic setting, and multiple interpretations from the past centuries. A thought-provoking feast for the eyes and the mind.
~ JANE DAGGETT DILLENBERGER, PROFESSOR OF ART HISTORY & THEOLOGY, THE GRADUATE THEOLOGICAL UNION BERKELEY, CALIFORNIA, AUTHOR OF *STYLE AND CONTENT IN CHRISTIAN ART: THE RELIGIOUS ART OF ANDY WARHOL*

Charles McCollough literally gives us a new perspective on Jesus' parables. McCollough's images are poignant, surprising, and oh-so-human. The accompanying text and questions help us experience these familiar teachings in fresh new ways – a living word for our day.
~ LOIS HUEY-HECK, CO-AUTHOR OF *THE SPIRITUALITY OF ART*

This beautiful intersection of words and images will engage the reader's imagination for the sake of both insight and transformation. What McCollough has produced is a parable in itself. Defying simple interpretations or pat explanations, it speaks to the spirit and the heart as much as to the intellect.
~ ROBIN MARGARET JENSEN, LUCE CHANCELLOR'S PROFESSOR OF THE HISTORY OF CHRISTIAN WORSHIP AND ART, VANDERBILT UNIVERSITY, AUTHOR OF *FACE TO FACE: THE PORTRAIT OF THE DIVINE IN EARLY CHRISTIANITY*

The Art of Parables

Reinterpreting the Teaching Stories of Jesus in Word & Sculpture

Charles McCollough

CopperHouse

Editor: Mike Schwartzentruber
Cover and interior design: Verena Velten
Proofreader: Dianne Greenslade

CopperHouse is an imprint of Wood Lake Publishing, Inc. Wood Lake Publishing acknowledges the financial support of the Government of Canada, through the Book Publishing Industry Development Program (BPIDP) for its publishing activities. Wood Lake Publishing also acknowledges the financial support of the Province of British Columbia through the Book Publishing Tax Credit.

BNC CERTIFIED | **BRONZE** | BIBLIOGRAPHIC DATA 2007-08

At Wood Lake Publishing, we practise what we publish, being guided by a concern for fairness, justice, and equal opportunity in all of our relationships with employees and customers. Wood Lake Publishing is an employee-owned company, committed to caring for the environment and all creation. Wood Lake Publishing recycles, reuses, and encourages readers to do the same. Resources are printed on 100% post-consumer recycled paper and more environmentally friendly groundwood papers (newsprint), whenever possible. A percentage of all profit is donated to charitable organizations.

Library and Archives Canada Cataloguing in Publication

McCollough, Charles R., 1934-
        The art of parables : reinterpreting the teaching stories of Jesus in word & sculpture / Charles McCollough.

Includes bibliographical references.
ISBN 978-1-55145-563-1

1. Jesus Christ–Parables. 2. Bible. N.T.–Criticism, interpretation, etc.
I. Title.
BS680.P3M33 2008   226.8'06   C2007-907578-9

Published by CopperHouse
An imprint of Wood Lake Publishing Inc.
9590 Jim Bailey Road, Kelowna, BC, Canada, V4V 1R2
www.woodlakebooks.com
250.766.2778

Printing 10 9 8 7 6 5 4 3 2 1
Printed in Canada by Houghton Boston

Table of Contents

Acknowledgements

I want to thank Sharon Ringe, Cathy Kapikian, Carroll Saussey, and Doug Lewis at Wesley Theological Seminary for their support at a turning point in my life when I phased out of my position on the national staff of the United Church of Christ into full-time artwork. Sharon launched me into the parables, and Cathy, Carroll, and Doug kept me going in the art studio at Wesley, newly enchanted with the art world as resident artist.

After that, Mark Burrows, Breta Gill-Austern, and Robin Jensen welcomed me into Andover Newton Theological School as resident artist and gave me many opportunities to exhibit my art, most recently the parable sculptures.

Charles Courtney, Heather Elkins, and Danna Fewell at Drew Theological School helped me to return to the holy texts of Jesus himself, the Hebrew Bible, and commissioned 11 sculptures for the seminary walls. Learning more of where Jesus' parables came from has enriched the last stages of this book.

Ursala Kapolitz, Doug Purnell, Wes Campbell, and John Carbone gave me many helpful critiques. Audrey Miller, always supportive, put me on to Wood Lake Publishing, where Lois Huey-Heck makes visual art a central part of the spiritual quest; and Mike Schwartzentruber edits with a thorough, careful, and helpful pen.

Most of all, my spouse, Carol McCollough, always ready to get me out of a computer tangle, edited and did countless other jobs to make this book and CD complete. To her I dedicate this effort.

Introduction

A Different Approach

This book with CD represents a different approach to the parables of Jesus. The first difference, and the most obvious one, is that I use *images*, specifically *sculptural images*, to reach back to what Jesus taught through the parables. I do this because I believe that what doesn't get through to us in words may get through to us in images; some things in our lives are "too deep for words," but not necessarily for images. Thus, the text and images combined may go where words alone cannot go.

The second difference from most other works on the parables is that my approach accounts for the economic and political context of Jesus' parables. To be sure, some parable scholars include this context when interpreting the parables, however, most of those who *do* limit the number of parables they discuss to a very few or they include no images. I will consider all of the major parables and most of the obscure ones.

Having said that, many parable interpreters completely ignore the economic and political context of first-century Palestine. When we include this context, the parables, which often are maddeningly mysterious, begin to make sense. I assume the spiritual and personal meanings usually given to parables, but add the economic and political issues as background. It is a both/and, not an either/or approach.

The Samaritan

Why Focus on the Parables?

But why should Christians focus on the parables rather than on other scripture texts? The answer is that the parables bring us as near to Jesus as we can get. Biblical scholars agree that the parables are the most authentic words available to us from the life of Jesus. While scholars interpret the parables in vastly different ways, and even the different gospels writers themselves disagree on the meaning of certain parables, recent research helps us get behind these conflicts to some of the historical realities of Jesus revealed in the parables.

Although the parables are not unique to Jesus, he made an art form of them, and some of his parables are almost universally known. The Samaritan and Prodigal Son parables, for example, are such a familiar part of world literature that they are used in endless ways to refer to the compassionate care of the stranger and to forgiveness of wayward sons. But are these the meanings Jesus intended? And what about the other 30 or so parables?

Prodigal Son

The parables are a direct route to Jesus, and we use them often not only for literary reference, but for preaching and devotions. They are listed over 30 times in the *Revised Common Lectionary*, challenging pastors over and over to interpret their mysteries. This is no easy job, because they rarely offer a single, clear meaning. Because of this mystery, the parables have enticed thousands of writers to try to find their meaning, even as some scholars deny that we can *ever* get a firm grasp of their message.

Parable Scholarship: A Brief Overview

Seeking to understand Jesus' parables is a joyous, wise, and daunting task. It is joyous because, as Amos Wilder says, "There is wide agreement that it is in the parables that we can feel confident that we hear Jesus of Nazareth speaking" *(Jesus' Parables*, 82). For Christians, the possibility of hearing Jesus' actual stories after 2,000 years represents something of a miracle, especially for those who are aware of the extensive editing done to Jesus' words, which were written down from memory some 40 to 55 years after his crucifixion.

The search for the meaning of Jesus' parables is wise because in them we may come close to the *basileia tou theou*, usually translated as "kingdom of God." I prefer "Empire of God" (which I capitalize), to account for the economic/political contrast to the "empire of Rome" (which I do not capitalize), and to account for the virtual demise of kingdoms in the West. There is scholarly consensus that the parables point mainly to the Empire of God. Jesus encourages us to strive for this kingdom (Matthew 6:33a, Luke 12:31), and we pray the Lord's Prayer, which contains a plea for its coming. Obviously, we need to have a clue about what that kingdom or empire is.

Of course, we discover quickly that trying to understand the parables is a daunting task, in part because Jesus often turns the question of their meaning back on to us: "Which of these... was a neighbour?" he asks the lawyer, and us, after he tells the Samaritan parable (Luke 10:25–36).

To complicate matters, after we separate the parables themselves from the gospel writers' *interpretations* of them, we often find that Jesus provided no clear application or interpretation himself.

But even if we take the gospel writers' interpretations of the parable, we have to decide which interpretation in which gospel we will accept, since the gospel writers do not always agree on their interpretations, as we've already pointed out. Take, for example, the parable of the Great Supper (Luke 14:15–24; Matthew 22:2–10). In Luke's interpretation, the poor, crippled, blind, and lame are all welcomed, and only the excuse-makers are excluded from the food. In Matthew's interpretation, by contrast, a king sends a poorly dressed guest to hell, destroys murderers, and burns their city. Which interpretation do we follow: Luke's gentle exclusion from food, or Matthew's less-than-gentle exclusion from life and even after-life? We cannot have it both ways.

Such conflicts among the gospel writers and puzzlements about the meanings of the parables have led scholars and preachers to pen untold numbers of books, essays, and sermons. Mastering this extensive bibliography is a major task – daunting indeed.

We who start the journey through the parables will be further challenged even to define what a parable is and, thus, which of Jesus' sayings are actually parables and which are some other literary form, such as a proverb or example story. (See Bultmann's distinctions between figures, metaphors, similitudes, example stories, allegorical explanations, and parables [*History*, 166–205]). As well, most scholars now follow Adolf Jülicher, C. H. Dodd, and Joachim Jeremias in rejecting allegorical interpretations as true to Jesus' words, even though the gospel writers frequently interpret the parables allegorically. But there are exceptions. John Drury, for one, says that the gospel writers' allegorical interpretations are all we have, and that these interpretations are bound to their respective parables at birth. In other words, he claims that we cannot separate the parables from the gospel writers' allegorical interpretations of them (*Parables*, 2–3). Other scholars, such as G. V. Jones (*Art and Truth*, 24–25), take a middle position that affirms some limited allegorical application. (I provide more details on this in chapter two, where I take a position that only occasional words need to be used allegorically and symbolically, not whole parables.)

Virtually all parable scholars agree that, as opposed to being propositional, discursive, or abstract speech, parables are images or word pictures "drawn from nature and common life." As such, they draw concrete images that "tease it [the mind] to active thought" (Dodd, 5).

Such pictures or images have immediate efficacy in communication. They instantly communicate meaning from one person to another, as opposed to abstract, discursive, propositional language, which must reference an external, agreed-upon meaning code. We can see this difference in the following two examples. In Matthew 13:44, Jesus says, "The kingdom of heaven is like a treasure hidden in a field." In this example, the hearer immediately visualizes a treasure hidden in a field. But when Jesus says, "do unto others as you would have them do unto you" (Luke 6:31, Matthew 7:12), the hearer must consult the abstract codes of conduct contained in memory to imagine what behaviour may be relevant to oneself and to others. Images communicate concretely and immediately; wisdom sayings, such as the golden rule and other propositions, communicate abstractly and in a delayed fashion.

Verbal images not only communicate immediately, they stay in the mind. They last. In this book I am adding yet another challenge for the imagination in parable study. That is, I am taking the word images in the parables and making actual images of them. Through my clay images, I hope to reach deeply into the parables so that they may yield both immediate and long-lasting meaning. To *see* the meaning of a word or words is to reach a final and deeper level of understanding. We use the phrase "now I see," when we finally understand something. This priority of seeing over hearing is an ancient phenomenon. Hence, Job says to God as his cause of repentance, "I have heard of you by the hearing of the ear, but now my eye sees you..." (Job 42:05).

My hope is that although studying the parables can sometimes feel like a daunting task, you will experience it as a joyous one that may yield the wisdom of Jesus himself.

Not *Whether* to Use Images, but *How* to Use Them

I argued in detail in my last book, *Faith Made Visible*, why using visual images in worship and education is not only sound theologically, but critically important as a vital aspect and level of communication. I did this because the Protestant, Jewish, and Islamic traditions have long been suspicious of the power images hold and have rightly opposed the misuse of images in idolatry.

However, the misuse of words is also condemned in these traditions. The Ten Commandments contain two prohibitions against the abuse of words – taking the Lord's name in vain and bearing false witness – and only one prohibition against making images into idols (Exodus 20:4, Leviticus 19:4, Deuteronomy 4:6–18, 5:8). We can see idolatry of the word in modern times in the extreme reactions of people for and against the placing of stone carvings of the words of the Ten Commandments in U. S. court houses.

It is long past time that we, in Protestantism, put away iconoclasm and embrace images, as Catholic and Orthodox Christians have done since ancient times. As a Protestant, and indeed as one from one of the most iconophobic traditions of the Reformed churches, I realize that convincing scholars and church leaders to use images in seminaries, adult education, and worship is a challenge. Protestant seminaries are only beginning to experiment with the use of the arts in general and congregations move slowly when it comes to accepting new approaches. Yet I have been using images in seminary teaching and preaching for ten years, with notable acceptance and success.

The question now is not *whether* it is appropriate to use images in church, but *how* to overcome the barriers that would prevent their use and, once these are overcome, how to actually incorporate images in congregational life.

The pastor is called to the local church to preach the Word with words, not with images. Words are the central focus of all Protestant worship. The way we have constructed our theological semantics so that the same language is used for God's Word and our preached words tells us how close we have come to an idolatry of the word. We know, of course, that God is in no way contained in our words. Yet we let this ambiguity of God's Word and our own words stand. If indeed God's presence is known in words and in images and even in silence and in darkness, then we need to allow some space and time to seek that presence through sight as well as through sound.

Protestants by and large have done a good job in the disciplines of preaching and music. We have a rich tradition of hymnody and extensive structures for skilled, weekly musical contributions in worship services. God's presence is heard in sound, both preached and played. Here, I simply want to affirm that the logic that supports the use of visual art in our churches is the same as the logic that supports our use of music.

Great deference is paid in seminaries and churches to using the right words – written, spoken, played, and sung. Aramaic words, Greek words, Hebrew words, and homiletics: all of these discipline our minds and tongues to orthodox language. The tradition of sermon preparation (one hour preparation for every minute of preached sermon) is usually accepted, even expected, for pastors. Yet it is unusual if a seminary offers even a single course in art appreciation. We *do* have visual art in our church buildings, both in our sanctuaries and in our education wings, but it is often haphazardly pinned to bulletin boards. For the most part, visual art in our churches is treated casually in the extreme.

Paying Attention

Paying attention to God's creation is an imperative for religious people, but we rarely give it *visual* attention because most of our focus in churches is on reading, speaking, and hearing. As a start to integrating visual art into churches, art appreciation helps us make some critical distinctions between works by trained and amateur artists. Also a trained artist can be asked to teach art in a church just as a trained musician teaches music. This distinction is not elitism; we make this distinction in our choice of music and music leaders as a matter of course. To be sure, we encourage children to draw in church schools. But why do we stop doing so when they reach puberty? When I teach art classes to adults, many of them are terrified at the thought of trying to draw, as if shame and abuse will follow anything less than a perfect sketch.

Personally, I believe that I cannot really see things in this world *unless* I spend time sketching and drawing them. Sketching is how I begin to pay attention to the world around me. It amazes me what details appear in objects when I take the time to really see them well enough to sketch, draw, or sculpt them. For many spiritually inclined people, paying attention in this way is a form of prayer.

As we begin to pay attention, it's also important to note the difference between *seeing* and *glancing*. With the advent of film, video, and computer graphics, we have become trained to *glance* at images, rather than to *see* them. As a result, we need to help students and parishioners who are accustomed to *glancing* at art to actually *see* art, in the sense of paying due attention so that they can discern the depths of meaning a piece of art may hold. Art contains far more than we can see or appreciate at first glance. We have to help people get around noetic, left-brain abstractions – as when children draw from memory a person's head that is larger than its natural size – that come from glancing at art and not seeing it at all. I hope the printed images and CD included with this book can help such *real seeing* happen.

Biblical Illiteracy

It is well-known that most people have no knowledge of the parables beyond The Samaritan and The Prodigal. One friend, a seminary professor, refused to believe the Warring King parable was in the Bible until I showed him. I have written this book with this unfamiliarity in mind. I have also tried to avoid technical language. My goal has been to make this book as readable as possible, while putting the best of recent scholarship in lay language.

Using this Book and CD

Each parable study in this book starts with a question to which the parable speaks. The question is meant to engage the reader and the viewer in the dialogue about the meanings of the parable. Jesus himself often started a parable with a question, such as "What do you think?" (Matthew 18:12), or "Which one of you...?" (Luke 15:3). These questions are tools that can be used to engage a congregation or class struggling with the issues raised in the parables – which always have implications for people living today, even though they were asked 2,000 years ago.

The text of this book includes small prints of the parable sculptures so that individuals can study the images with the text. The CD gives an overview of the parables in each of the synoptic gospels. In group study and in worship, the projected CD images are needed so that all participants can view the images together. For this, a data or multimedia projector is required with a computer and a PowerPoint program. If one does not own such, they are usually available for rent or loan from a college or judicatory office.

The images of the parables can be projected during worship to accompany a sermon on a parable. In this way, hearers will have images that stick in the mind, helping them to remember the sermon. In educational settings, the same projection equipment is required and the same learning dynamic applies. Careful study of the visual images is needed to *see* the parables.

The text of the parable research is background to the images and needs to be studied by the preacher or teacher even if the congregation or class does not. Each parable study in this book begins with a visual overview (A New Image) followed by a critical study of the most recent scholarship (Parable Research). Realistically, not everyone will read this research or the more in-depth study in Chapter 1 on the definition of a parable. But it is essential for leaders to study the background to the images and the overviews in the text and on the CD.

Usually only one parable can be covered adequately during a worship service. Two, or a maximum of three, can be studied in a one-hour class. This includes an introduction and a discussion of the images as they are projected on a large screen.

The CD provides a visual overview of the parables in Luke, Mark, and Matthew, in the same order as the text, with the two exceptions of the Doorkeepers and Overseer parable and the Children in the Market parable. It is wise to plan one educational session on each of the gospel overviews. Then plan follow-up sessions on the individual parables. For example, a leader can plan a six- to eight-week course consisting of one hour a week on the parables of Luke. The first session might look like this:

1. Introduce the parables. (15 minutes)
   a. Explain the importance of the parables to Jesus' message.
   b. Present the definition of a parable as a metaphor or simile with a story.
   c. Explain how the gospel writers, Luke in this case, framed and sometimes allegorized the parables.
   d. Describe the economic and political context of Jesus' time in occupied Palestine, and that of Luke's time, about 85 CE after Rome destroyed Jerusalem and the temple.

2. Show the Luke parables CD. (22 minutes)
3. Discuss Luke's attitude toward Gentiles and toward Rome. (10 minutes)
4. Discuss the reasons Jesus used parables. (10 minutes)

This introduction in session one can be followed by future sessions that might follow an outline similar to the one below:
1. Introduce one parable. (10 minutes)
2. Have someone read aloud the parable at least once, while projecting the images of that parable on the CD. (10 minutes)
3. Discuss the parable using the questions in the text. (15 minutes)
4. Project and read the second parable. (10 minutes)
5. Discuss the second parable. (10 minutes)
6. Summarize and/or make assignments. (5 minutes)

~ 1 ~

Defining the Parable

The Barren Fig Tree

What do you think?
Why do the innocent suffer and the wicked prosper?

Luke 13:1–9

[1]At that very time there were some present who told him about the Galileans whose blood Pilate had mingled with their sacrifices. [2]He asked them, "Do you think that because these Galileans suffered in this way they were worse sinners than all other Galileans? [3]No, I tell you; but unless you repent, you will all perish as they did. [4]Or those eighteen who were killed when the tower of Siloam fell on them – do you think that they were worse offenders than all the others living in Jerusalem? [5]No, I tell you; but unless you repent, you will all perish just as they did."

[6]Then he told this parable: "A man had a fig tree planted in his vineyard; and he came looking for fruit on it and found none. [7]So he said to the gardener, 'See here! For three years I have come looking for fruit on this fig tree, and still I find none. Cut it down! Why should it be wasting the soil?' [8]He replied, 'Sir, let it alone for one more year, until I dig around it and put manure on it. [9]If it bears fruit next year, well and good; but if not, you can cut it down.'"

A New Image

Pilate commands the attack on innocent worshippers: a woman and a child.

A Roman soldier carries out this brutal order.

In the background, a barren fig tree symbolizes this morally barren act.

The owner and gardener debate if there is any hope for fruit, that is, hope for an end to the suffering of innocents, and for accountability for those who are responsible for that suffering. These images appear on side one of a two-sided relief.

On side two, a flourishing, fig-bearing tree symbolizes this hope for alternative, morally productive acts.

Daring to act in such a way, the gardener challenges Pilate to stop the attack.

The soldier walks away, leaving his sword, which is used to plow in the manure. Pilate cringes in the presence of this challenge.

Granted, this scenario is fanciful in the extreme, but most of the parables are fictional tales about an alternative empire, in which justice reigns and the innocent are vindicated. In my depiction of the parable, the fruit of courage produces a world where things are made right. The gardener points to the attacked woman and child lying on the ground. Pilate drops his sword, suggesting an end to violence.

The viewer is left with a choice. That choice is the answer to theodicy, the ancient question, "Why do the innocent suffer and the wicked prosper?" The answer is the same for both the innocent and the wicked: because we give the wicked impunity to attack the innocent. In God's Empire, we refuse to allow such impunity. It is our choice.

The Importance and Meaning of the Parables

The more I read in the vast library of parable scholarship, the more puzzling the parables become. But I learn over and over that, like a case study or a Zen koan, the parables are *meant* to puzzle or "tease [the mind] into active thought," as C. H. Dodd said in 1938.

A parable is a long metaphor or a short story, in the rabbinic tradition of the *mashalim* – which were parables, as well as sayings and proverbs, both with and without narrative – meant to challenge one to a different level of being. An example is the *mashal* of the prophet Nathan, in which Nathan challenged King David with his parable about a ewe lamb that was stolen from a poor man by a rich man, and by which the prophet led David to condemn himself (2 Samuel 12:1ff).

As metaphors or similes plus narrative, the parables presented everyday images that were intended by Jesus to reveal the Empire of God. Indeed, many parable scholars, such as Amos Wilder, whom I mentioned in the Introduction, claim that parables are the most direct way to Jesus himself. Wilder says that we are able to hear Jesus of Nazareth speaking in parables because "they come down through retelling protected by their shape and hardness like quartz nuggets in a stream" (*Jesus' Parables*, 82). John Dominic Crossan says that parables are the "ontological ground" of the life of Jesus, and that they "are cause not effect of his other words and deeds" (*In Parables*, 32–33).

Sallie McFague speaks of Jesus himself as the "parable of God" (*Speaking*, xv). Robert Funk says, "He who does not make the journey by parable has no means for travel" (*Language*, 198).

But as critically important as the parables are to the very being of Christians, we cannot finally interpret their meaning(s). Rather, "[We are] to be interpreted by the text, not the text by [us]," says Robert Funk (50). Like a metaphor, a parable, according to Funk, "induces a vision of that which cannot be conveyed by prosaic or discursive speech" (*Language*,

136). A parable "does not illustrate this or that idea; it abuses ideas with their propensity for censoring sight" (139).

The meaning of the parables lies beyond ideas, moral examples, and concepts, all of which foreclose their power. Rather than *foreclose*, parables *disclose*, reveal, and transform one's vision, making one *see* in a radically different way. As John Donahue says, "[parables] point beyond what is expressed to what is beyond expression" (13).

Even though many scholars judge the parables to be beyond interpretation, at least with discursive speech, there is no limit to scholars who do in fact try to interpret them. In his interpretative commentary, Bernard Brandon Scott confesses, "to write a commentary on Jesus' parables is almost a contradiction although many have tried" (419). Yet in this same book, Scott himself spends 418 pages interpreting the parables.

What enchants me – besides these extravagant claims about the parables as a direct route to Jesus and even to God – is that these things the parable scholars say about the parables being beyond interpretation and beyond verbal or written grasp are exactly what many artists say about visual art. For example, the great painter Matisse is often quoted as saying, "If I could say it in words, I would not have to say it with paint." We all have heard people say that something is "beyond words," or "You have to see it to believe it."

But what are scholars, teachers, and preachers of the Word to do, when words won't do?

Most parable scholars use words that refer to vision to talk about the parables. "Imagination," "seeing," "sight," and even "art" are words used to refer to the multiple meanings of the parables. Norman Perrin says that Christian tradition,

> has allegorized and moralized parables…to the point at which one
> can live with them and draw helpful lessons from them. But when
> one approaches the parables… one finds them almost impossible to
> live with. They constantly shatter and probe, disturb and challenge

in ways which are for me personally analogous to the impact of great art. Even if I owned Picasso's *Guernica* I could not hang it on a wall in my house... (200).

If parables are something other than discursive speech and are more like visual images that challenge us, why not study, teach, and preach the parables using visual images? This seems like an obvious tactic, especially if our goal is to get beyond hearing and reading *words* so that the parable can grasp and interpret *us!*

Thus, students of the *words* of the Bible will greatly benefit from studying visual images based on the figures of speech, word images, and verbal pictures the rabbis and Jesus used in the *mashal,* or parable.

Defining the Parable

Parables are metaphors or similes, plus narratives, usually with a surprise turn that points *towards* God's Empire and *away* from all other empires. This is the simplest definition of a parable, although some scholars dispute whether a parable must have a narrative. Some commentators include as parables metaphors without narratives, such as "You are salt of the earth" (Matthew 5:13, Mark 9:50, Luke 14:34). This and many other sayings have no narrative. In the New Testament, parables so defined total in the hundreds.

In this book, I limit my definition of a parable to metaphors and similes that have narratives pointing *toward* God's Empire and *away* from its opposites. As I said above, most such parables have a twist or an odd turn that grabs the listener's attention and requires him or her to respond.

The New Testament contains roughly 30–40 such parables. An exact count is not possible because some stories are borderline parables, such as the Last Judgement (Matthew 25:31–46). Also, counting only 30–40 parables does not distinguish the same or similar parables in different gospels. For example, I count the Two Debtors parable (which appears in

Matthew, Mark, and Luke) as one parable, although all three synoptic gospels have different versions of it and John has a narrative reference to the woman anointing Jesus. The Gospel of Thomas, discovered in 1945, has 14 parables that are similar to those in Mark, Matthew, and Luke. It provides a useful tool for comparison with them. It has only three unique parables: The Empty Jar, The Children in the Field, and The Assassin. John's gospel has no parables.

Thus, I use the rounded-off count of 33, which covers individual versions and some borderline parables. It also includes all of the major parables and many obscure ones.[1]

In the next sections, I give a brief history of recent parable scholarship and draw from it the tools I will use to analyze each parable in the rest of the book. Along the way, I illustrate the use of these tools as I examine the Barren Fig Tree parable. Finally, I conclude the chapter with a summary of these tools and how they can be used to discern the message Jesus may have been trying to communicate with each of the parables.

A Brief History of Parable Scholarship

Modern parable scholarship began at the end of the 19th century with Adolf Jülicher's radical examination of the parables. The critical step he took was to reject 19 centuries of parable interpretation history, during which the parables were read mostly as allegories. In an allegory, each character or thing is really just a symbol for something else. So, for example, one allegorical interpretation of The Barren Fig Tree says that the fig tree symbolizes Israel, the owner symbolizes God, and the gardener symbolizes Christ, who pleads with God to allow the tree another season to bear fruit, that is, for sinful Israel to repent. Dare we ask what the manure symbolizes?

Jülicher rejected not only these later allegorical interpretations, but he also rejected the many allegorical interpretations that are present within the gospels themselves, for example, the allegorical interpretation of The Sower (Mark 4:3–20).

In rejecting both the allegories contained in the gospels as well as later allegorical interpretations, Jülicher also challenged earlier theologians, such as Augustine, who provides another famous, or perhaps I should say infamous, example of an allegorical interpretation. According to Augustine, in Jesus' parable The Good Samaritan, the Good Samaritan represents Christ, the robbed man represents Adam, the priest and the Levite represent the law and the prophets respectively, the inn represents the church, and the innkeeper represents the apostles. Augustine's interpretation of this parable is often held up as an extreme example of the misuse of allegory. In allegory the codes or keys must be known to understand the parable. Without the code, one is lost.

Most scholars, though not all, now vigorously reject allegory. In her recent book *The Parables of Jesus*, Luise Schottroff says, "The sweet poison of allegorization has immunized readers of the Bible" (175).

C. H. Dodd carried forward Jülicher's attempt to get behind both the allegorical interpretations contained in the gospels and the other kinds of editing done by the gospel writers, so that we could finally hear the actual words of Jesus in the parables. His now famous definition of a parable, which I quoted in part in the Introduction, is a good summary and is often followed by other scholars.

> At its simplest the parable is a metaphor or simile drawn from nature
> or common life, arresting the hearer by its vividness or strangeness,
> and leaving the mind in sufficient doubt about its precise application
> to tease it into active thought (5).

In the Barren Fig Tree parable, "nature and common life" are "vividly" expressed in the image of a fruitless tree. The "strangeness" is seen in the political context of Pilate's brutal attack on the Galileans as they made sacrifices in the Temple, and in the tower falling on 18 people at Siloam. This context is presumably what prompts Jesus to tell the Barren Fig Tree parable in the first place. But he ends the parable abruptly without any obvious connection to the context and without any assurance that the owner will spare the fruitless fig tree as the gardener advised. This "strangeness" *does*, in fact, "leave the mind in sufficient doubt... to tease it into active thought."

Joachim Jeremias took the next step after Dodd in seeking to reconstruct the parables in their historical context. In his book *The Parables of Jesus*, he listed seven "laws of transformation" to account for how Jesus' message got changed by the gospel writers and by later interpreters in the "primitive church." What follows is a summary of these "laws" and an illustration of how I use of them as tools, in this case to analyze the parable of the barren fig tree.

1. *Elaboration*. The primitive church added contexts or frames (beginnings and endings) to the parables. The Jesus Seminar, for example, has judged that Luke added (or elaborated) the first six verses of the Barren Fig Tree parable in order to set the context and to stress the need for *all* to repent (Funk, Scott, Butts, 60).

2. *Transference*. The original audience for or targets of Jesus' parables were "transferred" to the Christian community. In other words, Jeremias understood that rather than being exhortations to new Christians, as Luke makes out in his interpretation, Jesus originally used parables as a way to counter his opponents' arguments.

3. *Shift to hortatory (i.e., the giving of advice and encouragement).* Rather than stress the end of the age, which had not come as expected, the early church preached to its members about their behaviour. Luke's interpretation of the Barren Fig Tree parable calls for behaviour befitting repentance rather than end-time bag-packing.

4. *The Gentile mission*. Luke, especially, stressed the mission to the Gentiles a generation or two after Jesus. Thus, repentance applied to them as well as to Jewish Galileans. This is one way Luke sought to cope with the delayed return of Jesus, the *parousia*.

5. *Allegory*. As mentioned above, allegory was used in the synoptic gospels to encourage good behaviour and to interpret history, as well as to blame the Jews for Jesus' death.

6. *Parables collected and fused.* Mark grouped the seed parables together, which had been floating about in the oral tradition for years. Luke grouped the Prodigal Son, the Lost Coin, and the Lost Sheep parables together. The Barren Fig Tree parable is grouped along with other parables, in the so-called travel narrative in Luke. Matthew grouped the Young Women, the Talents, and the Last Judgement parables near the end of his gospel.

7. *Parables given settings that change their meaning.* If Jesus meant the Barren Fig Tree parable as a call for repentance (a favourite theme of Luke's), then the setting of the Galileans' tribulation may fit. But perhaps Jesus intended something else. In the original context of Roman oppression, suggesting that the Galileans should repent would have been akin to "blaming the victim." More on this conflict later.

Jeremias used these "seven laws of transformation" to search out Jesus' original parables and their settings, free of the gospel writers' additions and editing.

In fact, there are more than just seven things that played a role in the transformation of the parables. For example, Jesus spoke Aramaic and the parables themselves were part of an oral tradition. Yet the versions we have in the gospels are all in Greek, the language of the New Testament. No matter how skilled the translator, the parables would have gone through an unavoidable transformation as part of the translation process. This, too, is something to remember as we seek to get behind the text to find the original context and words of Jesus.

Given the complexity and number of factors that influenced the biblical texts we now have, some of the more recent scholars working in the field doubt that we can actually recover the original settings. In one sense, according to them, the gospel record is all we have. Luise Schottroff, for example, takes exception to the attempt to get behind the applications or frames that the gospel writers put around Jesus' parables saying, "they are an integral part of the parables" (*Parables,* 104). For her, "It thus makes sense to unpack the parable – the narrative and the application together…" (104). She includes three parts of the parables in her interpretations: the narrative, the application, and the response. The response of the hearers and readers is evoked by Jesus' frequent questions, such as, "Do you think…these Galileans were worse sinners…?" (*v.* 2); and by the parables' frequent abrupt endings. In her book *Jesus of Nazareth*, which she wrote with Dorothee Soelle, she declares the attempt to distinguish authentic from inauthentic traditions "outdated scholarly fiction" (*Jesus*, 35).

Obviously, I don't agree with Schottroff on this last point, since this whole book represents my attempt to understand the parables within their original social, economic, and political context, and to do that, one has to get behind the frameworks used by the writers of the gospels. Thus, I find myself more in agreement with the work of Joachim Jeremias, as presented above, and with the modern scholar, Bernard Brandon Scott, when he calls the most authentic words of Jesus the "originating structure" and the gospel writers' re-telling of the parables "performances." In this view, we come to see the parables in the gospels as relative approximations of what Jesus may have said.

This World More than the Next

To return to our history of the development of parable interpretation, the next step in parable scholarship after Joachim Jeremias was taken in the United States by Amos Wilder. Wilder brought a literary background to parable study. He believed that Jesus used parables to cast a "spell" that had the power to transform the imagination with "action images" (*Jesus' Parables*, 81, 83). Wilder saw Jesus as a layman who used secular stories *without* mysticism, miracles, or general ideas, rather than as someone who wanted to communicate a literal or other-worldly or spiritualized message. Jesus set out "not to substitute another world for this one, but to redeem and to transfigure the present world" (75).

The Barren Fig Tree parable could hardly be more this-worldly. No distant world or future time is referenced. Rather, the audience or reader is simply presented with the vivid "action image" of a gardener pleading for one more season to apply manure so that the barren tree might bear fruit.

Parables as Pictures

Robert Funk and John Dominic Crossan continued Wilder's literary criticism in parable research and stressed the inability of discursive language to state definitively the meaning of *any* of the parables (Funk, *Language,* 141–142). Rather, the concrete images and word pictures in the parables function on the imagination, not to illustrate this or that idea, principle, or moral behaviour, but rather to change, disclose, and radically alter one's whole way of seeing and "comporting oneself" with reality (195).

For example, the parable of the barren fig tree starts with a simple picture of a real-life, real-world problem in Jesus' day (a tree that is barren). The audience of any era is quickly engaged in a picture story. The twist or curve follows when the listener or reader "discovers it is not his [or her] world after all" (162).

This Barren Fig Tree parable ends so abruptly that the audience is left hanging, the imagination reeling in the attempt to find an ending, a punchline, a conclusion, an application. In other words, Jesus leaves us to *figure* it out, that is, to create a figure, an image, a picture, or a vision for our own life.

The Empire of God

Norman Perrin declared that the kingdom of God is the "ultimate referent" of the parables of Jesus. As a metaphor, the parable "produces a shock [to the imagination] which induces a new vision of the world and new possibilities" (202).

Many scholars agree that the kingdom or Empire of God is the "ultimate referent" or focus of the parables, but many of the parables, including The Barren Fig Tree, do not mention it. To complicate matters further, some of the parables that *do* refer to the kingdom or Empire of God seem to compare it only to corruption.

Bernard Brandon Scott points out that disjunction and dissimilarity are often used in the parables, such as in the Leaven parable, where a woman puts leaven in three measures of grain. How could God's realm be compared to a baker woman and to unclean bread? We have to remember that leavened bread, a barren tree, and a barren woman were considered cursed in the Bible just as a fruitful tree, a fruitful woman, and unleavened bread were considered blessed. Scott suggests that Jesus often attacked such boundaries and conventional visions of the holy. Luise Schottroff calls these dissimilar parables "antithetical parables" (*Parables*, 104). They point to God's Empire by picturing another antithetical world that is "unclean."

This parable of the fruitless fig tree is such an antithetical parable – one that creates the hope that the tree will indeed become fruitful just as Sarah, by God's blessing, became a mother though she was previously barren. But *can* the barren fig really become fruit-bearing? Scott, like the parable itself, gives no clear answer, but says, "in the parable the ellipsis is the Kingdom" (Scott, 338).

Parables as Political Resistance

As a person deeply concerned about issues of peace and justice, I am amazed by how much is written about the parables (and about the whole Bible for that matter) that ignores or dismisses how politically and economically relevant they really are. It seems like even the most learned scholars tend to wear blinders when it comes to politics in the Bible. Of course, this is not true of all scholars. For example, Sharon Ringe, Barbara Reid, Steve Patterson, Walter Wink, Luise Schottroff, Richard Horsley,

Marcus Borg, Ched Meyers, and John Dominic Crossan *do* work with the political, economic context of the parables. But no one has delved more deeply into parables as political and "subversive speech" than William Herzog. He says in a caricatured critique of other parable scholars,

> The scenes presented in the parables were valued for their theological, ethical, or metaphoric value, and once this was established, the details of the parable were left behind. Given this basic orientation, it mattered little whether one operated with a moral generalization (Jülicher), a single theological theme (Dodd), a variety of theological themes (Jeremias), [an] existential theme (Via), or a philosophy of language and perception (Crossan, Funk). The fate of the social world or the social scripts glimpsed in the parable was the same: they were ignored or, after cursory examination, neglected (*Subversive Speech*, 13).

This is an overstatement, especially of Crossan, who, as I said above, *does* refer to political and economic issues in the New Testament, especially in his later works, such as *In Search of Paul*. But the big picture of parable research does find such political details missing.

In the context of the Barren Fig Tree parable, the statement that Pilate mixed Galilean blood with their sacrifices means he slaughtered Galileans in the Temple while they worshiped. That act was obviously a *political* act of state terrorism in the extreme. In our own time, I am reminded of Archbishop Oscar Romero, who was murdered during mass.

More recently Luise Schottroff has continued the economic and political perspective of Herzog, whom she says "offers a decisive, new beginning" (*Parables*, 98). She examines the economic, political, anti-Judaic, and patriarchal assumptions of the gospels and their later, dualistic interpretations, which often reflect Christian triumphalism.

In particular, I find her central theses of eschatology defined not as a linear end time but as the "expectation of the just judgment of God" (104) a productive concept in parable interpretation. Thus, when the gardener proposes to give the barren fig tree one more year to produce before the decision is made to cut it down, the expectation of fruitfulness, "the just judgment of God," is offered.

However, the political context of Jesus' parable, which includes Pilate's atrocity, is often considered a Lukan addition and/or an inevitable tragedy, a natural disaster that had no human causation and thus no possibility of change or political consequences. The 18 people killed by the fallen tower are also seen as fatally destined, as if no builder can be held accountable for its weak design.

This dismissal of human accountability, which began with Luke's own focus on personal repentance, is what Herzog, Schottroff, and a few others want to correct by including the political context in the study of the parables. To highlight perhaps the key political reality in all of the New Testament, we need only point out that Jesus would hardly have been crucified for his theological beliefs. Crucifixion was a punishment for those who threatened the Roman empire. Roman authorities could have cared less about Jesus as a spiritual guru.

> If [Jesus] had been…a master of the inner life…of spirituality…, he would have been supported by the Romans as part of their rural pacification program…magic, passivity before fate… Narrativity [storytelling] and metaphoricality [metaphor study] were not capital crimes in the Roman empire… He was executed as an enemy of the state (Herzog, *Subversive Speech*, 27).

Richard Horsley makes a helpful comment on the way we spiritualize Jesus and ignore his political and economic world. He compares our reading and writing about Jesus to studies of Abraham Lincoln and Martin Luther King, Jr. How absurd it would be if we read and wrote about Lincoln's and King's spiritual words and deeds without any mention of slavery, poverty, or war. Yet that is exactly what has happened to Jesus' words and deeds. Theologians have turned Jesus into a cosmic, otherworldly, and ahistorical figure who is concerned only with personal salvation and not poverty, slavery, or war.

As Steve Patterson says, "most of us will take personal salvation over the empire of God any day" (*Beyond the Passion,* 130).

Like John Dominic Crossan, N. T. Wright sees in Paul's letters a "deeply counter-imperial" and politically "subversive" challenge to "the whole edifice of the Roman Empire" (Wright, 44). The Empire of God, the central focus of Jesus and his parables, was a direct, treasonous, and obviously political affront to the Roman imperial cult.

The political setting for the Barren Fig Tree parable was the report of an atrocity of state terrorism, when Pilate attacked Galilean worshippers. When you think about it, it's amazing that this political piece of scripture survived at all. First, as textual critic Bart D. Ehrman emphatically says,

> Not only do we not have the originals, we don't have the first copies of the originals. We don't even have copies of copies of the originals, or copies of the copies of the copies of the originals. What we have are copies made later – much later. In most instances, they are copies made many *centuries* later. And these copies all differ from one another, in many thousands of places (10).

Add to this the fact that for many centuries it was the monarchs, from Constantine to King James who, despite the fact that they would not allow texts to directly oppose their empires, sponsored the translations and copying of the biblical texts, and you begin to appreciate how amazing it is that scripture still bears witness to God's Empire of love, justice, and non-violence in Jesus' parables!

In the case of the Barren Fig Tree parable, this survival may be explained by the fact that Luke framed the atrocity as an issue of personal repentance required of all. In other words, the suffering Galileans were no more guilty of sin than others who were not killed. This theological point – that the rain falls equally on the just and the unjust and therefore we all must repent – has been made over and over through the ages. And that is necessary, of course. But what is too often ignored is that the repentance Jesus called for is not only a *private* turning of one's life around, not only a *spiritual* turning toward another, otherworldly realm, it is also a *public repentance*. To be sure, repentance is a very personal change of life, but repentance *also* involves *public* accountability in this world. Pilate was "one of the most notorious thugs in the history of the Roman Empire," according to British scholar A. N. Wilson (57). He was "recalled to Rome by order of the legate of Syria, Vitellius, to stand trial for his vindictive savagery" (56). Pilate's atrocities, both against the Galileans in the Temple and against Jesus on Golgotha, must be accounted for, just as we must account for present-day atrocities. Otherwise, we followers of Jesus are as barren as the fig tree.

While Schottroff affirms the political context of this parable, she insists that we include each gospel's application (frame). In this parable, that application is Luke's call to repentance. For Schottroff, repentance does not mean conversion to Christianity nor does it mean "blaming the victim." Rather, it means "following God's Torah, what is just." Confronted with the "gigantic war machine of the Roman military," those who repent transform themselves from threatened victims into acting subjects. "They work for righteousness and law as intended by Torah" (*Parables*, 62). In other words, the repentance in Jesus' message is both a private and a public call.

Other scholars are beginning to include public as well as private interpretations of Jesus' parables, so that we can now begin to see Jesus' whole message as a call to God's Empire of personal *and* public peace, justice, and shalom. Regrettably, William Herzog does not interpret this Barren Fig Tree parable in his books, but Barbara Reid suggests that when we preach this parable today we include,

> the story of the undeserved slaughter of the Galileans [which] gives Christians courage to denounce officially sanctioned terrorism or exemplary violence used by political authorities to exercise control over captive peoples... Christian fruitfulness [like the fig tree] would be visibly measured by the ways in which Jesus' followers unmask the lies of perpetrators of violence and open a space for their repentance (*Luke, Year C*, 54).

Who can possibly deny that Pilate is guilty and is included in this call to repentance?

From the beginning of the New Testament in Paul's letters, Christians subtly opposed Rome's imperial theology and oppression. John Dominic Crossan points out that only Caesar claimed the titles "God, Son of God, God of Gods, Savior, Lord, Redeemer. When Paul and other early Christians called Jesus these names, it was 'calculated treason'" (*In Search,* 11). The first Christians withdrew from Rome's imperial theology and empire, and sought first and last the Empire of God, the central focus of the parables of Jesus, an act of traitorous sedition to Rome. In a word, the parables contain political acts, words, and symbols throughout. To ignore them is to miss their point.

Summary of the Tools for Interpreting the Parables

1. Go behind the gospels. The gospel writers often disagreed on a parable's meaning because they had different goals (theologies). In Mark 13:32–37 and Matthew 24:32–35, for example, Jesus teaches a "lesson" in which sprouting fig leaves are a sign of the coming of God's Empire. Luke does not include this "lesson." He does, however, include the Barren Fig Tree parable, which he frames as a story about repentance.

2. Stay flexible when declaring a parable's meaning. Jesus often left the parables open-ended. We do not have, for example, Jesus' interpretation of the Barren Fig Tree parable.

3. Look for God's Empire in the parables. Not all of the parables mention it, but they all point to God's Empire directly or indirectly, when they contrast it with conventional behaviour or wisdom or other empires.

4. Detect the public ("the nations") aspect of the parables. Beware of spiritualizing and privatizing the parables to the point that they become irrelevant to the major public issues of this world.

5. Translate symbols; beware of allegory. The parables use symbols, but extended allegories enchant more than they enlighten. They are "over coded."

6. Beware of blaming "the Jews." Responsibility for the death of Jesus, and for the deaths of other Galileans, clearly belongs to Rome and to the high priests who cooperated with Rome, not to "the Jews."

7. Look at the parables as secular stories. They are not about otherworldly, religious, or cosmic adventures.

8. Note that parables usually end with a twist. Though they begin with everyday objects or events, they usually end with a curve, sometimes even an irreligious one.

9. See parables visually. They are pre-conceptual, immediate picture stories.

10. Enjoy the parables as short, narrative fictions. The "lesson" of the other fig tree (Mark 13:32–37 and Matthew 24:32–35) is not a parable by my definition, because there is no narrative story. But both lessons and parables are fictions that teach the truth.

11. Prepare to make a decision. The goal of parables is not entertainment or intellectual rumination, but the commitment of the hearer to a new way of seeing and living.

12. See the parables as "subversive speech." They are about subverting the kind of power that is based on violence and injustice. Only God's Empire of justice, peace, and love deserves our allegiance.

13. Look for God's Empire to come not in lineal time but in the hope for justice *in all time*. Like the Galileans, all innocent victims of atrocities await the day when our faith will bear fruit, when we will have the courage to stand up for them against the tyrants of our age. When this happens, we will experience the real and present Empire of God. The parables, then, are narrative metaphors and similes that were originally meant to shock Jesus' audience out of their captivity to the empire of Rome. If we take them seriously, they will serve the same purpose today, by shocking *us* out of our captivity to the empires of the present age.

---

[1] Some scholars include sayings and borderline parables that I do not include because they only fit very loosely my definition of a parable, and they are very rarely studied by most scholars. However, my cut-off point is somewhat arbitrary. I will list here some of parables I don't include but that are included by some scholars: The Empty House, Matthew 12:43–45, Luke 11:24–26; The Weather Report, Matthew 16:1–4, Luke 12:54–56; The Undeserving Servants, Luke 17:7–10; The Narrow Door, Luke 13:22–30, Matthew 7:13–14; and The Places at the Table, Luke 14:7–11.

Parables in
the Gospel of Luke

~ 2 ~

The Children in the Marketplace

WHAT DO YOU THINK?
How do adults act like children when they reject God's Empire of
goodness, peace, and justice?

[18]The disciples of John reported all these things to him. So John summoned two of his disciples [19]and sent them to the Lord to ask, "Are you the one who is to come, or are we to wait for another?" [20]When the men had come to him, they said, "John the Baptist has sent us to you to ask, 'Are you the one who is to come, or are we to wait for another?'" [21]Jesus had just then cured many people of diseases, plagues, and evil spirits, and had given sight to many who were blind. [22]And he answered them, "Go and tell John what you have seen and heard: the blind receive their sight, the lame walk, the lepers are cleansed, the deaf hear, the dead are raised, the poor have good news brought to them. [23]And blessed is anyone who takes no offense at me." [24]When John's messengers had gone, Jesus began to speak to the crowds about John: "What did you go out into the wilderness to look at? A reed shaken by the wind? [25]What then did you go out to see? Someone dressed in soft robes? Look, those who put on fine clothing and live in luxury are in royal palaces. [26]What then did you go out to see? A prophet? Yes, I tell you, and more than a prophet. [27]This is the one about whom it is written, 'See, I am sending my messenger ahead of you, who will prepare your way before you.' [28]I tell you, among those born of women no one is greater than John; yet the least in the kingdom of God is greater than he." [29](And all the people who heard this, including the tax collectors, acknowledged the justice of God, because they had been baptized with John's baptism. [30]But by refusing to be baptized by him, the Pharisees and the lawyers rejected God's purpose for themselves.) [31]"To what then will I compare the people of this generation, and what are they like? [32]They are like children sitting in the marketplace and calling to one another, 'We played the flute for you, and you did not dance; we wailed, and you did not weep.' [33]For John the Baptist has come eating no bread and drinking no wine, and you say, 'He has a demon'; [34]the Son of Man has come eating and drinking, and you say, 'Look, a glutton and a drunkard, a friend of tax collectors and sinners!' [35]Nevertheless, wisdom is vindicated by all her children."

(See also Matthew 11:16–19.)

A New Image

How can we imagine this parable? My two-sided relief depicts the comparison of the children in the market on one side, and John and Jesus, wisdom's children, on the other side.

The children in the market are arguing with each other and refusing to play each other's games. They represent Jesus' generation under the rule of the Roman empire. The boys play flutes and taunt the girls, expecting them to dance. The girls wail, expecting the boys to join them in mourning. The tables and shopper in the distance identify the place as a market. A Roman soldier guards the marketplace, symbolizing Roman domination. The refusal to cooperate with each other suggests the squabbling divisions of "this generation."

On the second side, the ascetic John and the indulging Jesus both preach about another Empire. John is very thin from his diet of locusts and honey, he is a little wild-eyed, and he wears camel hair clothes.

As a result, this generation says, "He has a demon." John points to Jesus as the "one to come." His other hand guides the Roman soldier's spear away from his side.

Jesus is much more beefy as he eats regular food and drinks wine. He points to heaven, God's Empire, with one hand and holds a glass of wine in the other. He is called a glutton and drunk.

Although both John and Jesus were rejected and murdered by Rome, they were vindicated by the deeds of future generations, including the deeds of those of us who also follow the way of John and Jesus today.

Parable Research

This is a borderline parable. It has a comparison simile, which uses the word "like," but the narrative is minimal: children play the flute and wail, but are rejected by each other, just as John (who fasts) and Jesus (who does not fast) are rejected by "this generation." Also, there is no obvious twist to challenge its audience, unless one counts the rather confusing comparison of the children with John and Jesus.

Scholars judge that this parable and its interpretation come from the Q source, as the versions found in Luke and in Matthew are very similar. They are not identical, however. Luke 7:35 says "wisdom is vindicated by all her children," while Matthew 11:19 says "wisdom is vindicated by her deeds." If we follow most scholars, who favour Luke's vindication by children, then the parable contains two sets of children: squabbling children and wisdom's children. Joachim Jeremias points out that the children's play would have been flute-playing by boys, and wailing as at funerals by girls (121), though their gender is not specified in the text.

Many scholars skip this parable or ignore the political context in which it is set by the gospel writers. However, that context is highly charged with political acts of state violence, the ultimate method of Roman domination. Also, Matthew's version includes the telling sentence in verse 12, "From the days of John the Baptist until now the kingdom of heaven has suffered violence, and the violent take it by force." (Luke also has a similar sentence in 16:16.) John has been put in prison by Herod Antipas, where he will soon be murdered for judging Herod for marrying his half-brother's wife. While in prison before he was killed, John sent two of his followers to check out Jesus. Is Jesus the messenger of God's Empire or not? Jesus answers by citing deeds he has performed that are similar to those he is called to do in Luke 4:18. He heals the blind and sick, raises the dead, and preaches relief from poverty. In other words, he acts to carry out the promises of God's Empire.

Jesus then tells the crowd that John is more than a prophet. No one is greater than him, in spite of his rustic clothing and his ascetic lifestyle.

But many people find both John and Jesus offensive. Jesus, for example, is rejected by the lawyers and the Pharisees especially. In fact, the whole generation is offended by these messengers of God's Empire.

Then Jesus tells his parable. This generation is like squabbling children in the market. You can't please them. Whatever one group says, the other group rejects. Some play the flute, but the others will not dance to it. Some wail a dirge, but the others will not mourn with them. Likewise, this generation rejects whatever John and Jesus do, even though their lifestyles are opposites. This generation responds to John's way of fasting from bread and wine by calling him crazy, demon-possessed. But then, like squabbling children in the market, they respond to Jesus, who eats normal food and who drinks wine, by calling him a "glutton" and a "drunk." In addition, they ridicule him for cavorting with tax collectors and sinners.

Whatever they do, John and Jesus cannot please this childish generation. The graphic comparison looks like this:

Children in the market	Children in the market
Play the flute	Wail dirges
Others refuse to dance	Others refuse to mourn
Jesus takes food and drink	John fasts from food and drink
Jesus called a "glutton" and "drunk"	John called "crazy"

All are rejected: the children reject each other, and this generation rejects John and Jesus.

This reading assumes that the title "Son of Man" refers to Jesus in the third person. In other words, Jesus is simply saying, "I have come eating and drinking, and you say..." If the title is supposed to mean more than that, such as Daniel's "a human being coming with the clouds of heaven," an apocalyptic figure (Daniel 7:13–14), then this interpretation has probably been applied to the parable by the early church.

Other questions remain. Is this parable authentically from Jesus? Some say "yes," because John is placed on the same level as Jesus. Also, Jesus is called a "glutton and drunk." Neither description would likely have been written by the early church (Jeremias, 121). Others, such as A. T. Cadoux, say that the interpretation in the text does not fit the parable, which for Cadoux indicates that it is not from Jesus (32). Many other scholars agree that the parallel analogies between the children's dirges and the flute players do not match up with the interpretation of the ascetic John and the indulging Jesus. However, this lack of a fit does not argue against Jesus' authorship, in my opinion.

Scholars also debate other questions, such as whom do the children in the market represent: this generation who squabble, or John and Jesus who cry out but are ignored? There is no consensus on this question, but I find it more convincing to equate the squabbling children with this generation rather than with John and Jesus. For one thing, Luke often uses the term "this generation" in a similarly negative way in other places (see for example 9:41 and 11:29). Also, it is difficult to think of John and Jesus as quarrelling children. Rather, it is easier to see them as *wisdom's* children, which is in fact how Barbara Reid names them. In particular, she stresses the feminine aspect of God as wisdom, Sophia (*Luke*, 276–277). It is *this* wisdom of God that is vindicated by her messengers, John and Jesus. Matthew, of course, always insists on good deeds, and so has wisdom vindicated by her deeds.

This generation not only rejected John and Jesus' message, but murdered them. Yet God's Empire will be vindicated by all of these pairings: wisdom's children and wisdom's deeds, John and Jesus, and death and resurrection. The Roman empire killed John and Jesus, because it thought they were a threat to its rule. And so they were, because they preached allegiance to another Empire, that is, to God's Empire, which does not rule by violence and injustice.

Questions for Discussion

1. *How were John and Jesus similar and how were they different?*
2. *Have you ever had a "nothing pleases them" experience?*
   What was that like for you?
3. *Do you think our own generation also rejects God's Empire?*
4. *If so, what empires have we chosen instead of God's Empire?*

~ 3 ~

The Two Debtors

[36]One of the Pharisees asked Jesus to eat with him and he went into the Pharisee's house and took his place at the table. [37]And a woman in the city, who was a sinner, having learned that he was eating in the Pharisee's house, brought an alabaster jar of ointment. [38]She stood behind him at his feet, weeping, and began to bathe his feet with her tears and to dry them with her hair. Then she continued kissing his feet and anointing them with the ointment. [39]Now when the Pharisee who had invited him saw it, he said to himself, "If this man were a prophet, he would have known who and what kind of woman this is who is touching him – that she is a sinner." [40]Jesus spoke up and said to him, "Simon, I have something to say to you." "Teacher," he replied, "speak." [41]"A certain creditor had two debtors; one owed five hundred denarii, and the other fifty. [42]When they could not pay, he cancelled the debts for both of them. Now which of them will love him more?" [43]Simon answered, "I suppose the one for whom he cancelled the greater debt." And Jesus said to him, "You have judged rightly." [44]Then turning towards the woman, he said to Simon, "Do you see this woman? I entered your house; you gave me no water for my feet, but she has bathed my feet with her tears and dried them with her hair. [45]You gave me no kiss, but from the time I came in she has not stopped kissing my feet. [46]You did not anoint my head with oil, but she has anointed my feet with ointment. [47]Therefore, I tell you, her sins, which were many, have been forgiven; hence she has shown great love. But the one to whom little is forgiven, loves little." [48]Then he said to her, "Your sins are forgiven." [49]But those who were at the table with him began to say among themselves, "Who is this who even forgives sins?" [50]And he said to the woman, "Your faith has saved you; go in peace."

A New Image

It is a challenge to imagine this parable because it is situated within a larger story, and it directly interacts with that story. As I explain in the parable research below, I interpret both the parable and the story as a lesson in *seeing*. Jesus directly rebukes Simon and his blindness by asking him if he *sees* the woman.

So that the reader/viewer will see the woman clearly, I have put her front and centre and in three dimensions on side one of the two-sided piece. She is there, full figure, for all to see, as compared to Jesus and Simon, who are in two-dimensional relief. She is caressing Jesus' foot; an empty jar of ointment supports her arm.

A real challenge for me was representing the debt, an abstraction that is interchangeable with sin in the Bible. As in the Unforgiving Slave parable (pages 205-210), I have cut out a negative space in the shape of a money bag. It is negative money or money one does not have. That is, debt money is present, but negatively so.

Jesus lifts that debt off the woman as she honours him with kisses, shaming Simon who did not show any such honour or hospitality. The parable within this story makes the point that the greater the debt forgiven, the more the debtor or sinner will love the one who offers the forgiveness. Jesus' question to Simon requires him, indeed traps him, into acknowledging as much.

On the first side of the sculpture, I depict Simon as being offended as well as blinded. On the second side of the sculpture, he is shocked. The Two Debtor parable connects to the meal at Simon's house, because, like the woman, Simon is also a debtor, represented by the negative space or debt/sin above his head. Unlike the woman's debt, however, Simon's debt remains unlifted by Jesus, because Simon is blind not only to the woman, but also to his own debt/sin.

In contrast, on the second side of the sculpture, the woman is full of joy as she rises from her prone position to her knees.

Having known forgiveness, she can now love others.

Parable Research

First, we need to untangle some confusion caused by the fact that there are four similar gospel stories.

It is easy to mix up Luke's version with the stories in Mark (14:3–9), Matthew (26:6–13), and John (12:1–8). In Luke's version, this parable is placed inside the story of Jesus' visit to the house of Simon the Pharisee. The story itself illustrates the parable, which in turn influences the story's ending. In the Mark and Matthew versions, a woman anoints Jesus' head, not his feet, as in Luke and John. This anointing takes place in Bethany in the three other gospels, not in Galilee, as in Luke. Jesus is a guest in Simon's house in Luke, Mark, and Matthew, but a guest in the house of Lazarus, and of his sisters Mary and Martha, in John's story. Luke's Simon is a Pharisee, not a leper as in Mark and Matthew; and he is obviously not Lazarus, as in John.

There are some clear overlaps in the stories, suggesting that Luke adapted Mark's version and John adapted Luke's version, but there is no scholarly consensus on this. Numerous scholars consider Luke's version to be independent.

The most harmful confusion comes from John's version, with the association of Mary in that story (whom I'll call Mary of Bethany) with the "unnamed woman" in the other gospels. However, there is no evidence that the unnamed woman in the synoptics was Mary of Bethany in John's version, and it is not clear, whoever she was, that she was a prostitute. To complicate matters further, Mary of Magdala (a devoted disciple unrelated to either the "unnamed woman" or Mary of Bethany) has been confused with Mary of Bethany. And *that* Mary has been confused with this unnamed woman for centuries. Thus, Mary of Magdala has been assumed to be a prostitute, without any evidence to back up the notion. The "unnamed woman" is called a "sinner," but we do not know the nature of her sin, and it is not critical to the story or to the parable.

Finally, this parable of the two debtors in Luke is not to be confused with the parable of the two debtors in Matthew 18:23–35, best known as The Unforgiving Servant. The two parables are unrelated.

Now we need to consider the context of this parable. In order to get the full flavour of the powerful verbal battle between Jesus and Simon, we need to understand the customs, taboos, and social/religious/economic/political codes of the Middle East in Jesus' time.

Kenneth E. Bailey lived in peasant villages all over the Middle East and taught at the Near Eastern School of Theology in Beirut for many years. In his book *Through Peasant Eyes*, he shows that very little has changed over the centuries regarding the customs in these villages. As a result, we get helpful insights into why the encounter between Jesus, Simon, and the woman was so shocking.

According to the biblical text, Simon wants to test Jesus to see if he is a prophet, as has been claimed. So he invites Jesus to a banquet, where men (exclusively) discussed weighty matters such as prophecy. Jesus arrives for dinner and "reclines" for the meal and the discussion. (The NRSV English translation I've used above simply says, "took his place," but Kenneth Bailey, Barbara Reid, and others translate κατεκλίθή as "reclined.") Bailey says the fact that Jesus reclines suggests that the meal was a banquet, as reclining was a custom at banquets. We learn in verse 49 that other guests are present.

The food is placed in large dishes on low tables or on the floor, surrounded on both sides by low couches. Guests lean into the centre, with their bare feet (sandals and slippers are checked at the door) far away from the food for sanitary and aesthetic reasons. Over-exposure of feet and footwear is offensive in Middle Eastern cultures.

Before reclining, however, a guest was always met and greeted with a kiss on the cheek (for those of equal status), or on the hand (for those of higher rank). A bowl of water and towel were provided for guests to wash their feet. Oil for anointing one's head was often provided. The fact that Simon did not welcome Jesus with a kiss or water or towel or oil was a glaring omission for a host in a culture where hospitality was not only a custom but a religious duty. It was a "callous" and "deliberate" insult to Jesus that could not go unnoticed, according to Bailey.

Then the woman appears. Apparently, other villagers were allowed to observe these banquets. So the woman's presence as such was probably not an offence, but what the woman *did* was highly offensive to Simon's code of purity. Most offensive was that her response to Jesus was opposite to Simon's own insults. According to Bailey, who adds some drama to the scene,

> she witnesses the harsh insult that Jesus receives when he enters the house of Simon, as Simon deliberately omits the kiss of greeting and the foot-washing. The insult to Jesus has to be intentional and electrifies the assembled guests. War has been declared and everyone waits to see Jesus' response. He is expected to offer a few tight-lipped remarks about not being welcome and withdraw. Rather, he absorbs the insult and the hostility behind it and does not withdraw (8).

Perhaps having experienced Jesus' forgiving love before, or at least having heard him preach it, the woman boldly interrupts this gathering of men and responds in a fashion that is the exact opposite of Simon's insults. She offers Jesus her kisses – many kisses, not to his cheek or even to his hand, but more humbly to his feet. She provides the missing water by using her tears to wash Jesus' feet. With no towel provided, she shamelessly lets down her hair (grounds for divorce if she is married) and wipes Jesus' feet with it. With no oil for anointing, she offers her perfume or ointment for his feet.

Many commentators observe how sexually suggestive her behaviour was in a culture where any kind of touching in public between unmarried men and women was not allowed. But Simon holds Jesus especially accountable for allowing these gestures to continue in his house. This was enough evidence to answer Simon's test: "He said to himself, 'If this man was a prophet, he would have known who and what kind of woman this is who is touching him – that she is a sinner'"(v. 39).

Finally, Jesus speaks up with a blunt call to verbal battle. "Simon, I have something to say to you." But instead of a direct counter argument, Jesus throws Simon off guard with a parable. Rather than declare a proposition, Jesus, in typical fashion, asks a question, putting his opponent on the defensive and in a box: If two debtors are forgiven their debts, one of 500 denarii and the other of 50 denarii, which one will have a more loving response? Simon has to choose the greater debtor, but he does not seem to have his heart in his words, for he leads his answer with "I suppose." Jesus affirms his answer as the correct one. Then he turns to the woman and, according to scholars Mary Ann Bevis and Barbara Reid, asks Simon the "key question": "Do you see this woman?" Clearly, Simon cannot see her as anything but a sinner, and he cannot see Jesus as anything but a phoney prophet.

Then Jesus spells out his scathing rebuke of this self-righteous host at the same time as he affirms the woman. For a guest even to comment in any but complimentary terms on a host's hospitality is disgraceful in the Middle East. Bailey reports, "To attack the quality of hospitality offered, regardless of the circumstances, is unknown in fact or fiction, in personal experience or in traditional story" (15). And Jesus lets loose.

> I entered your house; you gave me no water for my feet, but she has bathed my feet with her tears and dried them with her hair. You gave me no kiss, but from the time I came in she has not stopped kissing my feet. You did not anoint my head with oil, but she has anointed my feet with ointment (vv. 44–46).

Jesus has not only told a profound parable that reverses the order of sin and forgiveness, but he also applies it immediately in a powerful exchange that radically unmasks the oppression of women in particular, and also of those who are bound by what we call today "religious abuse." If love and forgiveness, compassion and kindness, inclusiveness and welcome are central to the gospel, then exclusion, rejection, hatred, and demeaning of others based on gender and class are clearly antithetical to Jesus' message.

I affirm the focus on the central question, "Do you see this woman?" Jesus saw her as a forgiven, loving person. Simon saw her as an intruding sinner. The parable is intended to change how we *see*; that is, we are to see others *as people in their own right, capable and worthy of love*, and not merely as sinners or as outcasts.

Seminars for discussing issues of the day, symposiums on this and that, papers read and critiqued – all of these have their place. But Jesus seemed to attract outrageous party crashers and to enjoy causing a ruckus himself. The whole point is seeing differently. To emphasize this message, Jesus might have said to Simon, "*See*, it is not what you think. *See*, it is what she *does*. Can't you *see*?"

Clearly, seeing differently is the first essential step to opening up to God's Empire.

Questions for Discussion

1. *How do our customs compare to these customs in Jesus' day?*
2. *With whom are church members today more likely to identify? Simon or the forgiven sinner who corrected Simon's lack of hospitality?*
3. *Two thousand years ago, Jesus challenged the abuse of women. What would she do now to support herself after she has left this "profession"?*
4. *Does it matter what the woman's "profession" was?*

~ 4 ~

The Samaritan

WHAT DO YOU THINK?
When can we receive aid from our enemies?

Luke 10:25–37

25 Just then a lawyer stood up to test Jesus. "Teacher," he said, "what must I do to inherit eternal life?" 26 He said to him, "What is written in the law? What do you read there?" 27 He answered, "You shall love the Lord your God with all your heart, and with all your soul, and with all your strength, and with all your mind; and your neighbour as yourself." 28 And he said to him, "You have given the right answer; do this, and you will live." 29 But wanting to justify himself, he asked Jesus, "And who is my neighbour?" 30 Jesus replied, "A man was going down from Jerusalem to Jericho, and fell into the hands of robbers, who stripped him, beat him, and went away, leaving him half dead. 31 Now by chance a priest was going down that road; and when he saw him, he passed by on the other side. 32 So likewise a Levite, when he came to the place and saw him, passed by on the other side. 33 But a Samaritan while travelling came near him; and when he saw him, he was moved with pity. 34 He went to him and bandaged his wounds, having poured oil and wine on them. Then he put him on his own animal, brought him to an inn, and took care of him. 35 The next day he took out two denarii, gave them to the innkeeper, and said, 'Take care of him; and when I come back, I will repay you whatever more you spend.' 36 Which of these three, do you think, was a neighbour to the man who fell into the hands of the robbers?" 37 He said, "The one who showed him mercy." Jesus said to him, "Go and do likewise."

A New Image

How do we communicate the parable of the Samaritan without words, but with images only? Some years ago, I made a sculpture of the Samaritan that I thought challenged the traditional interpretation. I made the Samaritan a woman coming to the aid of the beaten man. The sculpture was a response to the lawyer's question, "Who is my neighbour?" That was the theme of the Theological Institute at Princeton Seminary, where I had a sculpture show.

I thought that making the Samaritan a woman would counter some of the typical patriarchy in the Bible, but I still saw the parable from the helper/giver/Samaritan perspective rather than from the helped/receiver/victim perspective, which I now appreciate more after a careful study of parable scholarship. In other words, I saw the neighbour, the Samaritan, from the active care-giver perspective rather than from the passive care-receiver point of view. I have reversed that perspective in this book.

My new image of this parable is a two-sided combination of in-the-round and relief sculpture, and it takes a different perspective: that is, it takes the perspective of the *receiver* of the aid; the man beaten, robbed, and stripped.

I made the beaten man in-the-round, three-dimensional, and larger than the travellers who are in relief. They are two-dimensional and less easy to identify with. From the victim's perspective, we look up to the travellers – only one of whom stops to give aid. They are men of rank on a higher plane, fully dressed, and comparatively superior in every way, when measured by conventional standards.

Jesus' "answer" to the question "Who is my neighbour?" is a parable that traps us just as Nathan's story trapped David, as discussed in the Introduction. If we take seriously the fact that Samaritans were despised enemies of the Jews, then the neighbour should perhaps not be called the "good Samaritan," but rather the "bad Samaritan." In other words, if I identify with the beaten man – a more likely identification for Jesus' audience – then the Samaritan is an enemy from whom I must humbly accept help. In God's Empire, things get turned upside down so that *receiving* aid is as much of a blessing as *giving* it.

On side one of the relief sculpture, the priest and Levite pass by, while the Samaritan shows shock and compassion.

On side two, the Samaritan anoints the beaten man's wounds, mounts him on his horse, and takes him to an inn. The beaten man is passive and helpless. He must accept the aid, even from this Samaritan, who is an enemy.

Such humility must also apply to our interpretative efforts. We cannot assume our one view is *the* most accurate one, or the most true to Jesus' intent; we can never know, finally, the status of our interpretation. But at least this new interpretation traps us and forces us to the view from the roadside, where we must accept our enemy's offer of help. From this perspective, for which I credit Robert Funk (*Language,* 199–222), the message is not that the Good Samaritan is the good neighbour and that we should behave likewise, even if Luke interprets it thus.

Rather, the message is even harder to carry out. And that message is "love your *(enemy)* neighbour," even though you hate him.

Parable Research

The meaning of the parable traditionally known as "The Good Samaritan" seems clear and simple enough. Jesus appears to show an example of moral behaviour in which the Samaritan, unlike the priest and the Levite who pass by, stops and aids the wounded, robbed, and stripped man on the chronically dangerous road to Jericho. This interpretation has come down to us over the centuries and seems the obvious answer to the question, "Who is my neighbour?" The neighbour, or "my neighbour," is the one who serves the man in need. At least this is clearly Luke's perspective, because he adds, "go and do likewise" (v. 37).

Recently, however, scholars have noted that the lawyer asked Jesus a question concerning the commandment to love one's neighbour ("Who is my neighbour?") and received from Jesus no direct answer but rather a parable about an enemy (a Samaritan) and about a victim on a dangerous road that was rarely safe. (Roman legions had turned their attention elsewhere.)

It is not clear after all who the neighbour really is, or from what perspective one should read this parable. The traditional interpretation defines the neighbour as the "Good Samaritan," who gives aid to the victim beside the road. Naturally, we read this as a call to give the same kind of help to a wounded person.

But what Robert Funk and others have discerned is that the parable really focuses on the passive victim, as opposed to the active Samaritan. This is because Jesus' original Jewish peasant audience would more likely have identified with the beaten-down victim than with the Samaritan enemy. If we turn around the perspective of the traditional interpretation, it is the *receiver* of care, not the *giver* of care, who is the focus. That is, rather than seeing the parable from the Samaritan's point of view, which would be almost impossible for a Jewish peasant to do, we see it from the *victim's* point of view, which would be more natural to Jesus' listeners.

For first-century Jews, Samaritans were despised enemies, half-breeds, apostates, who deserved no respect from Jews, let alone the honour of giving aid to a Jew (assuming the victim is Jewish, though his identity is not revealed in the text).

Seeing the parable from the victim's perspective moves the interpretation from a moral example to a much harder challenge to love one's enemies, to experience the world of God's Empire where "we need our enemies to survive" (Patterson, *God of Jesus,* 151). Of course, Jesus wants his followers to aid those in need, but he also wants them to see the world from the bottom up and to know what it is like not only to *give* aid, but to *need* aid and to *receive* aid – aid given by one whom we view as an enemy.

Bernard Brandon Scott adds to Funk's and Patterson's interpretations by pointing out that the parable's use of the three travellers on the road from Jerusalem to Jericho would also have been an unexpected affront to Jesus' original audience. In the storytelling tradition of the time, Jesus' audience would have expected a threesome consisting of a priest, a Levite, and an Israelite or layman. We might compare a modern joke about a priest, a rabbi, and a preacher. However, Jesus breaks the expected series with a priest, a Levite, and a *Samaritan*. A comparable modern disjunction for us might be a joke about a priest, a rabbi, and a terrorist. This would have been a jarring incongruity for Jesus' listeners, though not for Luke's Gentile audience, who would have harboured no such expectations or any particular animosity toward Samaritans.

But if we look beyond Luke's interpretation, which sought to speak to the Roman world, and ask what Jesus was saying to his Samaritan-hating audience, then we are asked to do much more than follow a moral example. Jesus seems to be saying that God's Empire requires such a radical transformation that one must not only accept one's enemies (indeed, love them), but one must even be prepared to receive aid from the enemy – a most humbling gesture. Giving aid takes work, but receiving aid takes great humility.

If this interpretation comes closer to Jesus' original intent, then we (like Jesus' listeners) are called not simply to help the helpless, but to open ourselves to the possibility of receiving help from our most disliked rivals. Such humility and even deliberate weakness and foolishness (see 1

Corinthians 4:8–13 and "becoming like little children" in Mark 10:15) seems to be what Jesus demands of us, if we want to live in God's Empire.[1]

This call to "love your enemy neighbour" is more demanding than the traditional call to "help your neighbour." But it becomes even more challenging if we ask a political question: "Why was the road between Jerusalem and Jericho allowed to remain notoriously dangerous? Loving and receiving help from one's neighbour, as demanding as they are, can be seen as only private imperatives of personal morality. Yet the question must be asked, "Why, in first-century Palestine (and in 21st-century North America, for that matter), when the government had nearly limitless military power, was chronic lawlessness permitted in certain areas of the land and not in others? Why would Rome's vast military force permit such violence? Benign neglect, perhaps? My answer is: by keeping the ethical imperative focused on the private, neighbour, helper, the government was able to avoid its responsibility to keep all roads safe. Certainly, the mightiest empire of the time could have cleared the Jericho road of bandits, just as the mighty empires of today could make inner cities safe.

As always, the political question is hidden in the text, which was probably necessary for the survival of the text in the Roman and future empires.

The Samaritan parable looks different when seen from the victim's point of view, or from the Samaritan's point of view, or from the point of view of Luke's Gentile audience. It looks even more different when seen from the perspective of people whose land has been taken from them. I have been instructed in this perspective by a Native American, The Reverend Rosemary McCombs Maxey, *Mvskoke*/Creek, whose ancestral lands were taken during the Trail of Tears. She says of the Good Samaritan,

> As a person of color I am amused to think that there is only one – "The Good One." Of all the hated and despised and looked-down-upon Samaritans, there is The Good One. From where do you suppose The Good One learned to look beyond race, gender, class, ability and to thoughtfully care for others? I bet there's a good grandma Samaritan, a good grandpa Samaritan, and a few good

elders, a good number of the keepers and observers of the truth. They probably taught him to love God with all his heart, mind, and soul... The *Good* Samaritan does everything which is needed for the traveler/victim but no more: he takes care of him, brings him to an inn, feeds him, pays the innkeeper and then leaves the traveler/victim... He does not establish links of permanent aid, which would create dependence or aim at gratitude in the future.[2]

Rosemary Maxey shows how tokenism and dependency can flow from a skewed interpretation of the text.

To summarize, I believe that this very familiar parable can teach us that it is extremely wise to receive, learn from, and even be healed by our "enemies." However, that requires us to turn around the usual interpretation from the care-giver Good Samaritan, to the care-receiver who is aided by his "enemy." Then we can see what we need to receive, to learn, to be healed. Imagine how Euro-Americans could (and still can) learn and receive healing from native people, if we could only see from their point of view. How wise it would be to learn what radical Islam is all about.

Questions for Discussion

1. *Who is our neighbour today?*
2. *How does it feel to question Luke's interpretation of the Good Samaritan?*
3. *What do you think of changing the perspective from the Samaritan to the beaten man and to the displaced native person?*
4. *Which perspective would be more likely for Jesus' audience?*
5. *Why do you think the road between Jerusalem and Jericho was left unprotected?*
6. *How is dependence created?*
7. *Should we expect gratitude from people we help?*
8. *What can we learn from our "enemies"?*

---

[1] Note that the aid given to the man beside the road is a copy of the aid given to defeated Jewish captives by Samaritans in 2 Chronicles 28:14–15. After their defeat, Jews were brought with war booty to the Samaritan officials, but were then treated humanely after heeding the charge to do so from the prophet Obed. "They clothed all that were naked among them;...gave them sandals, provided them with food and drink, and anointed them; and carrying all the feeble among them on donkeys, they brought them to their kindred at Jericho, the city of palm trees. Then they returned to Samaria."

[2] Rosemary McCombs Maxey, "Dreaming of the Good Samaritan: A Postcolonial Perspective." A lecture given to the "Dream On Sisters" Women's Event, Indianapolis, IN, June, 24, 2006, Used by permission.

~ 5 ~

The Friend at Midnight

WHAT DO YOU THINK?
How far do you go to help a friend when you do not want to?

Luke 11:5–10

[5]And he said to them, "Suppose one of you has a friend, and you go to him at midnight and say to him, 'Friend, lend me three loaves of bread; [6]for a friend of mine has arrived, and I have nothing to set before him.' [7]And he answers from within, 'Do not bother me; the door has already been locked, and my children are with me in bed; I cannot get up and give you anything.' [8]I tell you, even though he will not get up and give him anything because he is his friend, at least because of his persistence he will get up and give him whatever he needs.

[9]"So I say to you, Ask, and it will be given you; search, and you will find; knock, and the door will be opened for you. [10]For everyone, who asks receives, and everyone who searches finds, and for everyone who knocks, the door will be opened."

A New Image

I imagine two main figures in this parable: a friend knocking and a sleepy villager who waves him away. I depict that image on the first side of a two-sided relief sculpture. The friend knocks with one hand and holds up three fingers on the other hand, for the three loaves of bread he is requesting. The villager is in bed and the window and door are closed. His children are in bed with him, as stated in the parable, a situation that would not be uncommon in an impoverished village, where a home may have only one room and maybe only one bed. The groggy villager appears crabby for having been awakened, but also because the intrusion would awaken his children.

Although it is not in the scripture, I added the distressed children on side two, as a natural consequence of the disturbance at midnight. Also on side two, the villager has opened the door to give the three loaves to the friend, who receives them.

These two images show how good deeds of hospitality are done in spite of one's attitude and regardless of how inconvenient it may be. The crabby villager comes through with the bread, even though he does not want to, and even though he will now have to get the children back to sleep.

Parable Research

This parable is found only in Luke, although there are similar sayings about seeking, knocking, and finding in Matthew (7:7) and elsewhere in Luke (12:36).

Luke surrounds the parable with prayer. He begins chapter 11 with the Lord's Prayer and ends it with sayings on how prayers are answered. Thus, persistence in prayer seems to be the theme of the parable.

However, a number of interpreters have questioned whether Jesus meant this parable to be only about prayer, especially *persistent* prayer. David Buttrick, for example, seeks to "correct the impression that we must pray all the time urgently or God will not respond. God is not a sleepy friend who does not want to get up in the night" (187). Buttrick goes on to note that the parable is also about hospitality, which was a "non-debatable obligation" in Jesus' day. Even so, he sticks with Luke's general focus on prayer.

Barbara Reid agrees that Luke "would seem to advocate badgering God until one gets one's wish." But, in contrast to Buttrick, she advises preaching on the theme of "extravagant hospitality rather than persistence in prayer. The parable was probably not about prayer in its original telling; it is Luke who gives it that cast with the surrounding literary context" (*Luke, Year C*, 131).

The idea that hospitality rather than prayer is the true theme of this parable is confirmed by William Herzog (*Subversive Speech*, 194–214) and others. They point out, for example, that hospitality was a critical survival strategy in village life. It is hard to overstate the pressure that was placed on village subsistence farmers by the urban elites who were caught up in the Roman economic and political oppression. Villagers were so over-taxed that many lost their land or were threatened with such loss – a situation that led to tenant farming, day labour, and possible starvation.

Extravagant hospitality – expressed as mutual sharing, or the obligation to share whatever one had – was one means by which poor villagers could attempt to ensure their survival. Such hospitality had also long been part of their cultural and scriptural tradition. In Genesis 19:1–11, for example, Lot goes so far as to offer up his daughters to a mob that is threatening to harm his guests, who happen to be angels/sojourners. To welcome strangers was to welcome "angels unaware," as confirmed much later in Hebrews 13:2. The part of the Torah that stressed social justice never lost this obligation of hospitality, whereas the part of the Torah that stressed purity focused on other obligations more convenient to the urban elite, such as tithing "mint, dill and cumin" (Matthew 23:23, also Luke 11:42).

It might seem strange to us that a friend would ask for fresh bread at midnight, but in a first-century peasant village, such a scenario would not have been uncommon. Although it's not explicitly stated in the parable, we can assume that the friend is asking because he is entertaining a guest. Everyone in the village would have been committed to feeding the guest the freshest and best food they could offer. The fact that the guest arrives late in the evening would also not have been unusual. Night travel was a common way to avoid the heat of the day.

Further evidence that all this was common behaviour comes from the actions of Jesus and the disciples, who often simply showed up in a village and asked for help.

Of course, in spite of the cultural, moral, and economic reasons for doing so, we can also understand why the sleeping villager might not want to oblige the friend knocking at midnight. Who, after all, appreciates being awakened from sleep, or relishes giving away valuable food? But the villager eventually does this, and therein models in his behaviour, if not in his attitude, the extravagant hospitality of God's Empire.

God's Empire often calls us at inconvenient times, when we do not feel like responding. But behaviour speaks louder than attitudes or words. Ultimately, the friend understood that welcoming the stranger was necessary, and so he acted accordingly. Likewise, the villager gave the bread, even though he was only half awake and he would have less food for his family the next day.

This rather mundane story stands out more when we see it against the contrasting background of the urban elites, who gave expensive feasts to impress other elites, and who "mimicked the behaviour of their Roman overlords" (Herzog, *Subversive Speech*, 213). These elites, like many well-off people today, would ask why the villagers did not hoard their meagre rations rather than risk starving or becoming dependent on the rich for handouts. The elites showed off their wealth with the conspicuous consumption of their reciprocal feasts, while they preached to the poor about thrift and hoarding their food.

From the villagers' and Jesus' perspective, of course, such small acts of mutual sharing are examples of the great banquet in God's Empire. At that banquet, no one goes hungry or thirsty, and all – especially the poor, the crippled, the blind, and the lame – are welcome.

Questions for Discussion

1. *Why would some scholars doubt Luke's interpretation of persistence in prayer?*
2. *What is the difference between persistent prayer and "badgering" God in prayer?*
3. *How often should we ask God for things?*
4. *Explain how the parable may be about hospitality and survival.*
5. *Rate the relative importance of attitude, words, and deeds.*
6. *How do we use food and meals to order our social worlds and commitments?*

~ 6 ~

The Rich Farmer

WHAT DO YOU THINK?
Should we share our abundance?

Luke 12:13–21

[13]Someone in the crowd said to him, "Teacher, tell my brother to divide the family inheritance with me." [14]But he said to him, "Friend, who set me to be a judge or arbitrator over you?" [15]And he said to them, "Take care! Be on your guard against all kinds of greed; for one's life does not consist in the abundance of possessions." [16]Then he told them a parable: "The land of a rich man produced abundantly. [17]And he thought to himself, 'What should I do, for I have no place to store my crops?' [18]Then he said, 'I will do this: I will pull down my barns and build larger ones, and there I will store all my grain and my goods. [19]And I will say to my soul, 'Soul, you have ample goods laid up for many years; relax, eat, drink, be merry.' [20]But God said to him, 'You fool! This very night your life is being demanded of you. And the things you have prepared, whose will they be?' [21]So it is with those who store up treasures for themselves but are not rich towards God."

(See parallel in The Gospel of Thomas 63.)

A New Image

The image this parable inspires in me is a two-sided relief. On one side is a close-up of the satisfied face of the rich farmer daydreaming in his soliloquy.

He dreams of taking his ease in a hammock strung between two palm trees. He holds up a drink, even as he plans to build bigger barns to secure his wealth and future comfort, because of his abundant crop.

Behind his head near the envisioned barns are the haunting images of the poor, which he does not see.

On side two of the relief, he lies in a coffin, which echoes the hammock. Two potted plants stand in for the natural palms that held his hammock on side one. The figures of the poor can be seen emptying the barns, illustrating the stern irony and foolishness of ignoring the poor while securing one's own wealth and comfort.

Parable Research

There is much disagreement among scholars on the meaning of this parable. Though most believe that the core of the parable comes from Jesus, almost all believe that Luke added the special concerns for the poor in the introduction, and the lesson at the end. That is, Luke added the question of the division of the inheritance among siblings before the parable itself, and added the moral after the parable. That moral is a warning that the rich farmer's fate is death before he can enjoy his riches. Such a fate awaits whoever is "not rich towards God" (v. 21).

Comparing Luke's version of this parable with a shorter version found in the non-canonical Gospel of Thomas (63), which does not have these additions, helps confirm this redaction by Luke. Thomas' version contains no direct speech by God, who in Luke calls the rich man a fool, and who declares his fate. (Luke's words from God are the only direct appearance of God in any of the parables.)

The common interpretation of this parable is simple enough. From Luke's own perspective, one should not be greedy. Greed, as expressed in the storing up of wealth into bigger barns, is foolish because death awaits, and because the rich farmer thinks only of himself and of his future life of ease, in which he hopes "to eat, drink and be merry" (v. 19). Luke's question in verse 20b suggests that the man will not leave an inheritance: "And the things you have prepared, whose will they be?"

The self-centredness of this farmer is evident in his soliloquy, in which he speaks only of himself. (Soliloquies are frequent in Luke and they are unique to his gospel.) Thus, he probably has no one with whom to share his wealth. The common view that "You can't take it with you" – there are no U-Hauls at funerals, after all – is the obvious reading of Luke's version, but this message and its "don't be greedy" corollary are not the only possible interpretations of the parable.

Charles Hedrick, for example, argues that there is nothing wrong with such enrichment or with the farmer's plans to enjoy it and be secure. The farmer is only acting as a not-too-shrewd businessman (157). Rather, Hedrick says it is the farmer's foolish mistakes that are the problem: not preparing earlier for the large crop, tearing down barns before building new ones, and not accounting for the possibility of his death (160). Hedrick also sees Luke's "stereotyped" view of the rich fool as "anti-upper class" (163).

David Buttrick takes quite the opposite view. He shows how "In the Bible, wealth is given [by God] for sharing, but the rich farmer is stocking up goods to guarantee his own pleasant future. He is revelling in profit while forgetting the poor" (189). The whole point of storing produce was to help the community, especially the poor, get through times of famine. Barbara Reid points out how the rich farmer thinks:

> The soliloquy...reveals his greed and his isolation. That the man talks only with himself is startling in view of the concept of dyadic personality out of which Palestinians of the first century operated. One's self-identity is imbedded in that of one's family, clan, village...
>
> The rich man, by contrast, has no thought of God or other people, planning to take his ease and indulge himself in food, drink, and merriment (*Luke, Year C,* 137–138).

In the early Jewish tradition, as with Joseph in Egypt, abundant crops were seen as gifts from God to be "harvests for the poor" (Buttrick, 189). Indeed, there is the suggestion that the phrase "your soul will be demanded of you" (*apaitousin,* v. 20) means that a debt is called in, as in the collecting of a loan (Donahue, 178). Thus, it is the poor (God's special people) who are calling in, if not this man's soul, at least some of his abundance.

Following this line of economic-political interpretation, the parable goes beyond the private warning not to be greedy and not to count on taking it with you. Rather, it considers the whole economy of wealth, property, and poverty, and suggests that greed is not just a private vice, but a public problem needing public solutions – for example, laws of inheritance and tax policies that limit the concentration of wealth, especially when it squeezes out the poor.

1. *How would you distinguish a private/individual interpretation from a public/political interpretation of this parable?*

2. *Do you agree with Charles Hedrick about Luke's "anti-upper class stereotype"?*

3. *Do you agree with David Buttrick or Barbara Reid about greed and the obligations of abundance?*

4. *How does the parable apply to customs and laws of inheritance today?*

~ 7 ~

The Doorkeepers and the Overseer

WHAT DO YOU THINK?
Will the Creator be happy with our care of creation?

Luke 12:35–46

[35]"Be dressed for action and have your lamps lit; [36]be like those who are waiting for their master to return from the wedding banquet, so that they may open the door for him as soon as he comes and knocks. [37]Blessed are those slaves whom the master finds alert when he comes; truly I tell you, he will fasten his belt and have them sit down to eat, and he will come and serve them. [38]If he comes during the middle of the night, or near dawn, and finds them so, blessed are those slaves.

[39]"But know this: if the owner of the house had known at what hour the thief was coming, he would not have let his house be broken into. [40]You also must be ready, for the Son of Man is coming at an unexpected hour."

[41]Peter said, "Lord, are you telling this parable for us or for everyone?" [42]And the Lord said, "Who then is the faithful and prudent manager whom his master will put in charge of his slaves, to give them their allowance of food at the proper time? [43]Blessed is that slave whom his master will find at work when he arrives. [44]Truly I tell you, he will put that one in charge of all his possessions. [45]But if that slave says to himself, 'My master is delayed in coming,' and if he begins to beat the other slaves, men and women, and to eat and drink and get drunk, [46]the master of that slave will come on a day when he does not expect him and at an hour that he does not know, and will cut him in pieces, and put him with the unfaithful."
(See parallels in Mark 13:32–37 and Matthew 24:45–47.)

A New Image

What images for the Doorkeepers and the Overseer parable will say it best? How can we both hear and *see* the call to carefully keep God's household, by properly distributing food and water, and by serving others in our care? I have tried to communicate these parables by comparing two images. My two-sided relief illustrates the two opposite servants as the master returns home.

On one side, the good doorkeepers (servants) have remained alert and welcome the master back into his home, which they have tended responsibly and have kept in an orderly fashion.

On the other side, the master arrives home to a very different scene. He opens the door himself to find that the overseer has abused his trust.

The negligent overseer is abusing the others in his care, as well as the drink and the food. The place is a mess and the returning master is shocked and angry, and reaches for his knife.

Parable Research

This double parable goes by many names, such as "The Returning Master," "The Waiting Slaves," "The Faithful and Wise Servants," "The Watchful Servants," and "A Man on a Journey." To add to the confusion, a number of other parables have similar master/servant themes. In particular, Mark 13:33–37 and Matthew 24:45–51 contain parallels with Luke. Mark has a brief doorkeeper parable that stresses the reward for alertness while the master is away. Matthew focuses on the overseer, using nearly identical wording as Luke, although Luke's version is longer and includes the doorkeepers and the overseer together. I am linking the two in what I will call a double parable, as they represent two sides of the same warning to stay responsible while the master is away.

In the verses about the doorkeepers, the doorkeepers stay responsible and are rewarded extravagantly – the master honours them by serving them a meal. Barbara Reid calls this master's service a "startling twist"; it's "a totally absurd scenario that a master would have his vigilant servants recline at table and then wait on them" (*Luke Year C*, 150).

The overseer part of the parable presents the opposite scenario, in which the servant in charge of the master's house takes advantage of the master's absence to eat, drink, get drunk, and beat the other servants, whom he is supposed to oversee. His punishment is so severe that translators soften the Greek word *dichotom`esei,* which literally means "to cut in half," saying instead that he is "severely punished" for his duplicity.

One other piece of helpful background is Kenneth Bailey's correction to the assumption that only the rich have servants. Bailey points out that "the poorest of the poor let their children out as servants so they can be fed, and people of very little means have such servants in their homes" (*Peasants,* 115). Also, the rich may have slaves and servants who attain very responsible positions supervising other servants, and managing whole estates and the wealth of aristocratic families, as in the Unforgiving Servant parable. These master/servant arrangements were the norm in

Jesus' time, and even the poor in his audiences would have been able to relate to them easily.

John Dominic Crossan counts eight servant/master parables, not including Luke 17:1–10, which he considers to be a proverb, not a parable. Of these eight, he points out that half of them have a conventional message or result, where good behaviour is rewarded and bad behaviour is punished. Some, however, seem to contain the opposite message or result. In these, bad behaviour is rewarded, such as in the parable of the dishonest steward. Crossan's point is that, in these latter parables, Jesus set up the conventional reward-for-good-behaviour and punishment-for-bad-behaviour scenarios, and then reversed and shattered their "normalcy" or conventional wisdom. God's Empire "shatters…our wisdom and prudence," he says (*In Parables*, 120).

Of course, this particular parable happens to contain a conventional message of reward for good behaviour and punishment for bad behaviour.

The synoptic gospel writers went further, however, and interpreted Jesus' parables, deeds, and stories from their much later point of view, 70 to 85 years after his death. They had expected Jesus to return, the *parousia*, but he had *not* returned, at least not in the sense they had expected. So they interpreted the good doorkeepers and the bad overseer to fit the later context of their waiting churches, who still expected the master, or Christ, to return at any time. Thus, their emphasis on diligent waiting and service.

In between the two parts of this double parable, Luke inserts the question from Peter asking for whom the parable is intended (v. 41). But Jesus does not answer directly. Rather, he tells the second half of the double parable. Thus, scholars are left to debate who the intended audience is. Arland Hultgren, for example, concludes that

> by virtue of having located that parable within the Travel Narrative (Luke 9:51 – 19:27), in which Jesus is instructing the Twelve for the time beyond his earthy ministry, it applies to others beyond the circle of the Twelve, including leaders of the church in Luke's own day (165).

Whether or not Jesus was actually preparing the disciples for "the time beyond his earthly ministry," we assume that the parables apply to all people, including us today, or else why would we have preached them throughout history and continue to do so today.

So what can we make of such a parable when after 2,000 years the *parousia* has not yet happened? Jesus has not physically returned, as the gospel writers and Paul thought he would, and, in a sense, we are also still waiting. But diligent waiting, as such, may just be Jesus' point.

Bernard Brandon Scott has a helpful insight here. Like Crossan, he relates this servant/master parable to other servant/master parables and observes that in all of them the master's "departure is a test and the return is an accounting" (211). In this parable, the overseer takes advantage of the master's absence because he fails "to realize that the kingdom is now – something with which he is entrusted" (212). Therefore, Scott asks, what if Jesus' continued absence, the delayed *parousia*, is a test not only for the early church, but also for us today. What would that mean? Scott does not spell out an answer, but it is worth pursuing, because we face the same temptation today as the overseer did then – that is, to ignore the test. Without the presence of anyone to hold us accountable – a judge or a community or a conscience – we easily do what the overseer did. We eat until we are obese; we drink until we are drunk; and we destroy other people in wars near and far. We also pollute the air and the water, and we destroy the land and the hope of future generations for peace and well-being in God's household.

Assuming this parable is for everybody, including us today, it could not be more timely. We have a clear choice, to be either the alert doorkeepers or the abusive overseer of God's household. Assuming we want to be the alert doorkeepers, we will show this by doing our duty to God by caring for the least among us. We will feed the hungry, provide clean water to those without it, and end violence towards others in all ways possible. In this way we will embody God's Empire now, in our own time.

If this interpretation of the Doorkeepers and the Overseer parable seems self-evident, consider how popular Christianity often claims to be waiting for the second coming of Jesus, all the while living like the overseer. Stephen Patterson bluntly says,

> We are killing Jesus... His words and deeds mean little to us, if anything at all. We do not look to Jesus for a way of life, but for salvation. "He died that we might live." Indeed. It seems we have to kill him in order that we might live whatever lives our power and privilege will allow us to lead. When real life is at stake, most of us will take personal salvation over the Empire of God any day (*Beyond*, 130).

There are those within Christianity who constantly preach personal salvation rather than God's Empire. There are many who emphasize the need to have a personal saviour and the importance of being "born again," while ignoring the least of our brothers and sisters. For some, this is even big business.

But for Jesus and for the early Christians, "the empire of God *was* salvation" (130). Perhaps the *parousia*, the return of the Lord, involves *our* return to God's Empire of care and justice, rather than the return of an individual person who is the personification of that Empire. Jesus called us to God's Empire, not only to himself. Or perhaps they are the same thing.

Questions for Discussion

1. *In what sense has Jesus returned or not returned to the disciples or to us?*
2. *Does the lack of Jesus' literal/physical return place obligations on us? If so, what are they?*
3. *What does it mean to say that the delayed* parousia *was a test to early Christians, or that it remains a test to us?*
4. *Name ways we care for or abuse the household of creation, which has been placed in our trust.*

~ 8 ~

The Great Supper

WHAT DO YOU THINK?
What excuses do we make for rejecting God's Empire?

[15]One of the dinner guests, on hearing this, said to him, "Blessed is anyone who will eat bread in the kingdom of God!" [16]Then Jesus said to him, "Someone gave a great dinner and invited many. [17]At the time for the dinner he sent his slave to say to those who had been invited, 'Come; for everything is ready now.' [18]But they all alike began to make excuses. The first said to him, 'I have bought a piece of land, and I must go out and see it; please accept my apologies.' [19]Another said, 'I have bought five yoke of oxen, and I am going to try them out; please accept my apologies.' [20]Another said, 'I have just been married, and therefore I cannot come.' [21]So the slave returned and reported this to his master. Then the owner of the house became angry and said to his slave, 'Go out at once into the streets and lanes of the town and bring in the poor, the crippled, the blind, and the lame.' [22]And the slave said, 'Sir, what you ordered has been done, and there is still room.' [23]Then the master said to the slave, 'Go out into the roads and lanes, and compel people to come in, so that my house may be filled. [24]For I tell you, none of those who were invited will taste my dinner.'"

(See parallels in Matthew 22:2–10, Thomas 64.)

A New Image

What does this parable look like? I see another two-sided relief with a dining hall. The hall is seen (cut away) inside and out, with the servant calling the invited guests, who are rejecting the call and making excuses one after the other. These excusing words can't be spoken in visual art, of course, but must be expressed in gestures and in body language.

The host is sitting, dejected, with head in hands, because he has been gravely insulted by his reneging guests. He is wondering what to do with all the food he has prepared. This is side one.

On side two, he decides to call in the street people. We see servant ushering in the street people, the poor, the crippled, the blind, and the lame.

A large group of disabled people line up to enter the feast. One is carried on a stretcher. Another blind person is led in.

The host has forgotten the insults and extravagantly welcomes all the street people to the great supper. The hall is decorated with garlands, and food is stacked on the low tables. The host, having broken all of the conventional rules, welcomes his guests, just as God welcomes all peoples into God's Empire.

Parable Research

Celebrating great events with a feast is a universal custom. In Jesus' time, feasts were used to maintain and solidify community bonds, beliefs, and futures "at table." Jesus even told this parable of the great supper while at a meal, after an unknown follower burst forth with, "Blessed is anyone who will eat bread in the kingdom of God" (v. 15).

Meal-eating customs were (and often continue to be) a microcosm of the social structure. For example, paternalism was constantly reinforced by the custom that only men could eat together at public banquets. The Great Feast came to be the symbol in the Bible for the ideal of shalom on earth, for God's Empire, when God's rule of peace and justice would reign. Note one model of such a feast in Isaiah 25:6–8.

> On this mountain the Lord of hosts will make for all peoples a feast of rich food, a feast of well-aged wines, of rich food filled with marrow, of well-aged wines strained clear. And he will destroy on this mountain the shroud that is cast over all peoples, the sheet that is spread over all nations; he will swallow up death forever. Then the Lord God will wipe away the tears from all faces, and the disgrace of his people he will take away from all the earth, for the Lord has spoken.

The symbol of God's Empire as a great feast continued in Jesus' parables, particularly this one. It is found in Luke, in Matthew, and in the non-canonical Gospel of Thomas, but is recorded very differently in each. The differences contained in each report reveal the agenda of each writer. Scholars judge Luke's version as probably closest to an original of Jesus, but Luke adds some of his favourite themes, such as "the poor, crippled, blind, and lame." He also adds a third call to the supper, and has the slave go beyond the city to the "roads and lanes" in order to fill the banquet hall. This is widely interpreted as a call to the Gentile world, a common missionary theme of Luke.

In Matthew's version, the servants who call in the guests are attacked. Matthew's host, who is a king feasting at his son's wedding, takes vicious revenge and destroys a whole city in his counterattack. Matthew also adds the punishment of a guest who comes to the supper improperly dressed, even though the hapless guest was abruptly swept in off the street.

Thomas adds a fourth guest who, like the other three, makes an unconvincing excuse for not coming to the feast to which he had previously committed himself. Thomas adds a merchant who is too busy collecting money to honour his pledge to come. Though Thomas does not allegorize the parable as Luke and Matthew do, he adds, "Buyers and merchants will not enter the places of my Father" (64).

Of the three versions, most scholars say that Matthew's is the most distant from Jesus, because of its weak credibility. (Why would a guest who is pulled off the street be properly dressed for a wedding feast of a king's son?) Also, Matthew allegorized the parable to fit his theme of salvation history, with each group in the story representing a group who rejects Jesus.

A great feast, as described in the parable, would naturally be given by a wealthy person who could afford it. In the rigid social structure of this period, an invitation would be given only to those of similar wealth and power – in other words, to those in one's class. The meal itself had to be prepared using meat slaughtered and cooked on the day of the feast. So there was some urgency to the second call to come, for "the meal is ready."

It was a serious offence, then, to reject the call to a feast, even with excuses. Many scholars go into great detail about how lame the excuses really are (Bailey, 95–99). To pick only one excuse: only a fool would buy a pair of oxen without inspecting it first. But this person claims he must inspect five teams he has already bought without inspection. The story gets more humorous, but it is so true-to-life that Jesus' audience can say, "Yes, this is what happens in real life." And they can laugh at such foolishness.

But then something unheard of occurs in Jesus' parable. The host commits what Barbara Reid calls "social suicide" (*Luke, Year C,* 314). He breaks ranks and has his servant call in the poor, crippled, blind, and lame off the street. Such breaking of class barriers simply was not done then (and is rarely done now, for that matter). This turn of events shocks the hearers, especially after the "comic criticism" of the weak excuses (Funk, *Language*, 195).

Jesus' listeners were likely smiling, if not laughing, at the excuses that made no sense, but Robert Funk makes a much bigger point of it than a few laughs. By ridiculing the wealthy excuse makers, Jesus

> debunk[s] the "going" understanding of the everyday situation. It exposes the pretensions of the prevailing way of comporting oneself with reality. In so doing it challenges the authority...by ridiculing it (195).

And the comic criticism opens "the way for a radically new disposition to reality, a disposition that is marked by the tragicomical" (195–196).

Suddenly, the everyday story of a jilted host is turned into a political satire. The conventional world of the host and of his "equals" is made to compete with the other world of the street people for a seat at the great supper, the very seat of blessedness in the Empire of God.

Oddly enough, most scholars ignore the economic and political conflict of these two worlds. But it seems obvious to me that the parable affirms the street people (and the tax collectors and the sinners) who are first in God's Empire, both in this parable and in many others. Jesus seems to declare that the wealthy are so stuck in their class and its customs that they cannot even imagine God's Empire, symbolized by the Great Feast.

By the sudden and unheard-of breaking of class conventions, the host and the parable teller catch the listener in a tragic-comical turn. "Where do I fit?" the listener must ask. "With the socialites or with the street people?" There is no way to earn admission to the Great Supper. It is a gift offered to "all peoples" and "all nations," to use Isaiah's words. That gift can and is rejected, especially by the wealthy, so that they are left out by their own choice.

The meaning of the third invitation in Luke's version to "Go out into the roads and lanes, and compel people to come in..." (v. 23) is much debated. After the poor, crippled, blind, and lame are brought in, the servant says there is still room. So the host tells the slave to *compel* people to come.

The most common interpretation of the third invitation is that it represents Luke's addition of Gentiles, the so-called "Gentile mission." A second and most destructive interpretation or application of the word *compel* has been the use of force or coercion to convert people to Christianity, something that has been tried often in the violent history of Christian imperialism. A third reading of the meaning of *compel* is less forceful and more sensitive to Middle Eastern customs. Kenneth Bailey points out that such an invitation to an upper-class feast would automatically be initially refused by outcasts, as a matter of courtesy. However, they may accept if the host insists – in other words, *compels* them to come (108).

A fourth interpretation I heard from Steve Patterson in a sermon. He turns the word *compel* away from assertiveness to attractiveness. That is, the Christian community should be compelling, *attractive*, to outcasts, even beyond the charity it offers to the poor, crippled, blind, and lame.

Such an invitation would go beyond charity to challenge the church to include *real* outcasts, such as lepers in Jesus' time, or gays and lesbians in our time.

There is no scholarly consensus on how to interpret the word *compel*, though the last interpretation is, for me, most challenging and consistent with Jesus' preaching of God's Empire.

Questions for Discussion

1. *How was feasting used as a way to solidify social bonds in Jesus' time? And now?*
2. *Does the symbol of the Great Feast work for you as a symbol of God's Empire? Why or why not?*
3. *Do you think the invitation to the street people was charity, justice, or both?*
4. *How do you interpret the master's order to "compel people to come in" to the feast?*
5. *In what ways might the church make itself more compelling to outsiders?*

~ 9 ~

The Tower and The Warring King

WHAT DO YOU THINK?
What does it mean to count the cost of discipleship?

Luke 14:25–33

[25]Now large crowds were travelling with him; and he turned and said to them, [26]"Whoever comes to me and does not hate father and mother, wife and children, brothers and sisters, yes, and even life itself, cannot be my disciple. [27]Whoever does not carry the cross and follow me cannot be my disciple. [28]For which of you, intending to build a tower, does not first sit down and estimate the cost, to see whether he has enough to complete it? [29]Otherwise, when he has laid a foundation and is not able to finish, all who see it will begin to ridicule him, [30]saying, 'This fellow began to build and was not able to finish.' [31]Or what king, going out to wage war against another king, will not sit down first and consider whether he is able with ten thousand to oppose the one who comes against him with twenty thousand? [32]If he cannot, then, while the other is still far away, he sends a delegation and asks for the terms of peace. [33]So therefore, none of you can become my disciple if you do not give up all your possessions."

A New Image

Although there is one clear message in both parables – count the cost of discipleship – the visual depiction of these two parables requires at least three images. On the first side of a two-sided relief, I depict a proud tower builder holding up a plan or blueprint of a tower, posing with an erect, even strutting confidence.

That he is *not* counting the cost is represented by his partner/spouse, who by her weary facial expression and posture suggests he is off on another big plan he will never finish. She is saying, in effect, "Here we go again with another one of his half-baked ideas!"

On the second side of the relief, events have played out as she knew they would. The tower has collapsed into ruins. The man sits despondently, his head on his left hand, his trowel dangling from his right hand. He is mocked with derisive laughter by the woman. The message is clear: count the cost of discipleship.

Though the second parable communicates the same message, how to depict it was not immediately clear to me. I spent a very long time trying to think of an image of a king going to war with or without counting the cost. My imagination searched for pictures of kings, warlords, dictators, and heads of state who were planning or implementing a war, or parading after victory. The power of an image of a victorious person entering into a community or a city can hardly be overstated. John Dominic Crossan characterizes the Greek and Roman generals' arrival in a city after victory not only as a military or political event, but as a religious event, a *parousia*.

> In its ancient context *parousia* meant the arrival at a city of a conquering general...or, above all, the emperor himself... It is probably necessary in those cases to translate *parousia* not as "visit," but as "visitation" (*In Search,* 167).

Then it hit me. The image of the U.S. president parading on the aircraft carrier under a banner that read "Mission Accomplished" seemed to fit, for such an "entry." Even though it was directed at a television audience, it was obviously meant as a kind of victory lap celebrating a mighty conquest. And yet as of this writing, years after he declared victory, a war is still raging in Iraq with no end in sight. Now legions of pundits and military advisors of all political persuasions have declared that the president never "counted the costs" before going to battle. As a result, many thousands are dead or wounded, and hundreds of billions of dollars have been wasted. A clearer example of a head of state not counting the costs would be hard to find. The corruption trailing behind this proud, warring "king" represents the now-obvious deceptions that were used to sell the war in the beginning.

Parable Research

Luke pairs these two parables just as he does the Lost Sheep and the Lost Coin, and just as Matthew does the Hidden Treasure and the Pearl. The Tower and the Warring King are unique to Luke. Scholars disagree on their origin. Some deny they are from Jesus (Funk, Scott, Butts, 68–69); others claim they are from Jesus (Hultgren, 139). Unlike many parables, these have a clear-cut application, with no twist or abrupt turn at the end of the parable itself. However, the call to martyrdom in verse 26 is a shock. Many parable scholars simply ignore these parables or make only brief comments on them, perhaps because the application is so evident.

Luke locates these two parables right after the Great Supper, where the invited guests find many excuses not to come to the feast of God's Empire. In this passage, Luke says those who think they want to follow Jesus toward the feast had better count the cost. Commentators usually soften the reference to "hating" and suggest that it means *secondary* to the primary commitment to Jesus. Thus, counting the cost means counting family and possessions, even one's life, as secondary to following Jesus on the way to the cross. To make the point as clearly as possible, two parables are told: both the tower builder and the warring king must count the cost before starting to act. If the builder cannot finish the tower, he becomes a laughing stock and is shamed. The unprepared king is defeated.

Barbara Reid points out that the first parable may have been a sly reference to Herod's vast building projects. If so, this would hint at a political meaning. Another possibility is that these parables are aimed at the rich, who have so much more to lose by putting everything – family, community, and possessions – behind the call to follow Jesus. The poor, of course, would lose few possessions.

Still, the injunction to put family and community second is shocking. The phrase itself comes before the two parables and is probably part of Luke's interpretation of them, since leaving one's family was not always demanded by Jesus. For example, Reid shows that Jesus instructed the

Gerasene demoniac to return home (Luke 8:39) rather than follow him, as the healed man wanted to do. Apparently, following Jesus to the cross is not for everybody.

The meaning of the Warring King parable seems to be the same – know the cost of your action before you start. Although not explicitly stated, any king who fails to do this before entering the battlefield may not only suffer shame, but death. Thus, the warring king who finds that his army is outnumbered two to one on the battlefield will surely sue for terms of peace. This could be a vague allusion to Jesus' saying about Jerusalem: "If you...had only recognized the things that make for peace" (Luke 19:42). Also, Luke could be suggesting that the Jewish revolt of 66–70 CE could have been avoided by a better counting of the cost, which turned out to be the destruction of Jerusalem and of the Temple.

Whether the parable is from Luke or from Jesus, the clear consensus among scholars is that the agreement to follow the way of Jesus requires going all the way. As Joachim Jeremias says, "a thing half-done is worse than a thing never begun" (p. 138).

Questions for Discussion

1. *What is the point of detecting Luke's editing or even his creating of these parables, as opposed to assuming that they come directly from Jesus?*
2. *How do you react to the verse that says we must "hate" family and possessions?*
3. *Does it make a difference to you that these might be the words of Luke and not of Jesus?*
4. *What are the costs of following Jesus today?*
5. *What, if any, costs have you had to pay to follow Jesus?*

~ 10 ~

The Lost Coin and The Lost Sheep

WHAT DO YOU THINK?
How does finding a lost valuable compare to finding God's Empire?

Luke 15:1–10

[1]Now all the tax-collectors and sinners were coming near to listen to him. [2]And the Pharisees and the scribes were grumbling and saying, "This fellow welcomes sinners and eats with them."

[3]So he told them this parable: [4]"Which one of you, having a hundred sheep and losing one of them, does not leave the ninety-nine in the wilderness and go after the one that is lost until he finds it? [5]When he has found it, he lays it on his shoulders and rejoices. [6]And when he comes home, he calls together his friends and neighbours, saying to them, 'Rejoice with me, for I have found my sheep that was lost.' [7]Just so, I tell you, there will be more joy in heaven over one sinner who repents than over ninety-nine righteous people who need no repentance.

[8]"Or what woman having ten silver coins, if she loses one of them, does not light a lamp, sweep the house, and search carefully until she finds it? [9]When she has found it, she calls together her friends and neighbours, saying, 'Rejoice with me, for I have found the coin that I had lost.' [10]Just so, I tell you, there is joy in the presence of the angels of God over one sinner who repents."
(See also Matthew 18:12–14, The Gospel of Thomas 107, and an obscure Gospel of Truth, which contains a second-century CE version of the Lost Sheep, in Arland Hultgren, 48.)

A New Image

There are two versions of the Lost Sheep parable in the gospels, as well as a version in the non-canonical Gospel of Thomas (107), and, of course, each is slightly different. I will focus on Luke's version because unlike the shepherd in the Matthew and Thomas versions of the Lost Sheep, Luke's shepherd "lays [the lost sheep] on his shoulders and rejoices" (v. 5). The image of a sheep on a shepherd's shoulder is an ancient one. In fact, the earliest known image of Jesus, found in the catacomb of Calistus (dated approximately 217 CE) is that of a shepherd carrying a sheep in this way. A shepherd with a sheep slung across his shoulders was a common image in the classical period of the Greco-Roman world.

In contrast to the parable of the lost sheep, the parable of the lost coin appears only in Luke's gospel.

The shepherd's care for the sheep and the woman seeking the lost coin are positive images of impoverished people who will risk everything (99 sheep) and sweep carefully (after the lost coin) to find the one thing of value that has been lost.

The shepherd in Luke's parable exhibits extravagant attention to the lost sheep and echoes the shepherd in Psalm 23 ("The Lord is my shepherd...") and in other Hebrew scriptures. Even though they don't include it in their own versions, the classical image of the shepherd carrying the sheep on his shoulders supports two themes common to Matthew and Thomas, as well as to Luke – that is, care for the least, and joy in finding them. Any images of the parable must communicate this joy.

The sculptural images I have created attempt to communicate this joy, which can be seen in the grinning faces. They seem to say, "It's time to party!"

The shepherd is presented initially in two images on a two-sided relief. On side one, he leaves the 99 sheep and sets off to the mountains after the lost one. A wolf howls on a distant mountain, suggesting the risk of leaving the other sheep. On side two, the lost sheep is found and the shepherd cannot be happier. This sculpture appealed to a number of people, so I also made an in-the-round version of it, shown here.

I depict the Lost Coin parable using an in-the-round sculpture, which focuses on the moment the coin is found and on the woman's joy at finding it. The broom and the lamp lie near her as evidence of her search. The woman relishes the precious coin, as she gazes at it close up.

Parable Research

I am considering these two parables together because Luke has grouped them thus. He also gives them – as well as the parable of the prodigal and elder sons – the same interpretation. Arland Hultgren has pointed out that, "It is somewhat typical of Luke to match a male example with one involving a woman" (64). Thus, the Lost Sheep and Lost Coin are considered "twin" parables, with male and female actors, and friends and neighbours to match in the two celebrations.

It is important to refer briefly to Matthew's and Thomas' version of the Lost Sheep, as they are both similar to and different from Luke's version. The similarity lies in the parable narrative itself, in which the shepherd or man leaves the 99 sheep to find the one lost sheep. But when framing the parable narrative, each writer has a different interpretation of Jesus' meaning.

Matthew begins with the warning, "Take care that you do not despise one of these little ones..." Then he ends the parable by comparing the little ones to sheep whom "your Father in Heaven" does not want to be lost – thereby essentially repeating his opening warning (v. 14).

In Thomas' version, the shepherd is compared with God's Empire, and it is the *largest* sheep that goes astray and is found, and that receives God's love even more than the 99.

Luke, by contrast, uses the parables of the Lost Sheep and the Lost Coin to stress the need for repentance. He also suggests that the Pharisees and the scribes are the lost ones, in contrast to the tax collectors and the sinners. The former condemn Jesus for eating with those whom the authorities declare unclean. Luke further emphasizes this theme of repentance with his interpretative statement, "there will be more joy in heaven over one sinner who repents than over ninety-nine righteous people who need no repentance" (v. 7).

Recently, scholars have found that the Lost Sheep parable itself probably originates with Jesus, but that these interpretations by Luke, Matthew, and Thomas were added later. Some point out that Luke's focus on repentance does not match the parable itself, because repentance is something a person must actively do, whereas neither a sheep nor a coin is active. They are both passive and the coin is a simple object. How can a sheep or a coin repent?

The search for Jesus' meaning in these parables, then, can go in a number of directions: 1.) with Thomas, interpreting the shepherd as God's Empire of extreme love for the best (i.e., the largest) of the lost sheep; 2.) with Matthew, as a warning to care for the little ones, as a shepherd would risk 99 to find one; 3.) or with Luke, who sees Jesus preaching repentance to the authorities and the scribes. However, these are not mutually exclusive options, for all of them point to three vital qualities: excessive love, attention to the lost, and joy in finding them.

Even in these parables of love and joy, there is an economic/political context. When Luke tells these parables, he is essentially suggesting to the Pharisees and the scribes that they imagine themselves as the main characters in the plot. In other words, they should imagine themselves as a shepherd or as a woman who has lost something; or they should imagine that God is a shepherd or a woman. Either way, the idea would have been quite offensive to them, since shepherds and women were considered unworthy. This insight makes it clear that Jesus was directly challenging the authorities, saying *they* are the ones who are really lost and in need of repentance, not just the tax collectors and the sinners. Once again, Jesus sides with the marginalized against the established authorities. And if we take the analogy further, it is the marginalized (the shepherd and the woman) who seek out, find, and save the well-off and the respectable.

But there's more. The woman, like the shepherd, is obviously impoverished, because she makes such a desperate search for a coin of limited value, although scholars debate its exact worth. The coin itself was a *drachma* (Greek) or *denarius* (Roman), both amounting to about a day's labour for a soldier or male day labourer. Male scholars usually rate the coin as having "little value" (Funk, *Five Gospels*, 355). However, feminist scholars point out that a woman would have to work two days for the same coin and would thus value it all the more, and would seek it most "carefully until she finds it"(v.8, Beavis, 36). The woman's careful search with a lamp (required in a dark and, therefore, most likely poor dwelling) and a broom also suggests that she was impoverished. Thus, Luke's Jesus not only identifies with the marginalized – with women, and with those who were seen as sinners or as unclean – he also identifies with the poor. Both, says Jesus, participate in God's economy, where women are equal to men, and the poor share in the wealth of the rich. No wonder the shepherd and the woman express such extreme joy! They have been found by God, and as a result, have discovered or experienced for themselves the Empire of God.

Questions for Discussion

1. *Which writer's interpretation of the Lost Sheep parable do you prefer and why?*
2. *Is the shepherd a positive or negative comparison to God/Jesus?*
3. *What images do you have of the Lost Sheep or the Lost Coin? How do we communicate love and joy without words?*
4. *How do you respond to the metaphor of God as a poor woman?*
5. *Why does Jesus side with the impoverished?*
6. *Is the joy of finding something lost comparable to finding God and/or God's Empire? If so describe such joy.*

~ 11 ~

The Prodigal and Elder Sons

WHAT DO YOU THINK?

Will unconditional forgiveness enable the prodigal to return to dissolute living again or will it convert him to responsible behaviour?

Luke 15:11–32

[11]Then Jesus said, "There was a man who had two sons. [12]The younger of them said to his father, 'Father, give me the share of the property that will belong to me.' So he divided his property between them. [13]A few days later the younger son gathered all he had and travelled to a distant country, and there he squandered his property in dissolute living. [14]When he had spent everything, a severe famine took place throughout that country, and he began to be in need. [15]So he went and hired himself out to one of the citizens of that country, who sent him to his fields to feed the pigs. [16]He would gladly have filled himself with the pods that the pigs were eating; and no one gave him anything. [17]But when he came to himself he said, 'How many of my father's hired hands have bread enough and to spare, but here I am dying of hunger! [18]I will get up and go to my father, and I will say to him, "Father, I have sinned against heaven and before you; [19]I am no longer worthy to be called your son; treat me like one of your hired hands."' [20]So he set off and went to his father. But while he was still far off, his father saw him and was filled with compassion; he ran and put his arms around him and kissed him. [21]Then the son said to him, 'Father, I have sinned against heaven and before you; I am no longer worthy to be called your son.' [22]But the father said to his slaves, 'Quickly, bring out a robe – the best one – and put it on him; put a ring on his finger and sandals on his feet. [23]And get the fatted calf and kill it, and let us eat and celebrate; [24]for this son of mine was dead and is alive again; he was lost and is found!' And they began to celebrate.

[25]"Now his elder son was in the field; and when he came and approached the house, he heard music and dancing. [26]He called one of the slaves and asked what was going on. [27]He replied, 'Your brother has come, and your father has killed the fatted calf, because he has got him back safe and sound.' [28]Then he became angry and refused to go in. His father came out and began to plead with him. [29]But he answered his father, 'Listen! For all these years I have been working like a slave for you, and I have never

disobeyed your command; yet you have never given me even a young goat so that I might celebrate with my friends. ³⁰But when this son of yours came back, who has devoured your property with prostitutes, you killed the fatted calf for him!' ³¹Then the father said to him, 'Son, you are always with me, and all that is mine is yours. ³²But we had to celebrate and rejoice, because this brother of yours was dead and has come to life; he was lost and has been found.'"

A New Image

This parable is relatively long and familiar, so I have made four in-the-round sculptures of it.

The first shows the prodigal squandering his inherited property. His dissolute living is evidenced by a bottle of wine in one hand and a bag of money in the other. Like most alcoholics, he creates wreckage all around himself without acknowledging it. Kegs of booze support his left leg and the wreckage supports his right. He is cocky and unaware of the messes he makes.

In the second image, the prodigal is in the pig sty. His emaciated figure indicates his dead-end condition, as well as the "famine in the land." He stares at the pig, jealous of the pods the pig has to eat. He has fallen to an animal level and is so passive he whines that he cannot even have the pig's food. He is lost. The pig stares back as if to ask, "What's your problem?" Unlike the prodigal, the pig is not lost but knows who he is and is content in his being, as expressed in his composure.

The third sculpture depicts the prodigal's return to his father, who smothers him with an embrace. The father is so happy that his lost son has been found that he almost crushes the starved figure. The prodigal is surprised at the reception and has a bewildered look, for he never gets to fully confess his sin, as he planned. His body is limp and his left hand is awkwardly caught in the embrace. In extreme contrast, the father is rotund, symbolic of a prosperous person. He has been shamed by both sons: the younger by asking for his inheritance before his death, and the older by refusing to join his father's celebration. And he has shamed himself by giving in to the prodigal's request. All of this shaming is based on the rules of the honour/shame society of that time, not on the rules of God's Empire.

Also, he runs to meet the son.

The fourth sculpture shows the father and the elder son, who has a petulant look and posture, as he refuses to come into his brother's party.

Again, the father goes out, this time to welcome the older son into the feast. He embraces him with one hand and motions with the other, "All that I have is yours."

The father welcomes both sons – one starved, shamed, and lost; the other well-fed, law-abiding, and obedient, but resentful of his brother's behaviour and of his father's forgiveness. Yet the father judges neither and rewards both by inviting them into the banquet.

Parable Research

This is perhaps the best-known parable next to the Samaritan, and both are found only in Luke. It deals with basic family issues of inheritance, sibling rivalry, shame, and forgiveness.

The mother of this family is glaringly missing, although some artists, such as Rembrandt, have included her in spite of her absence from the text. The absence of the mother or of any females in this parable is curious but suggestive of the powerful paternalism of the period and indicative of the economic and political context, which was controlled by the male head of a household. One scholar, Bernard Brandon Scott, sees the ever-forgiving father as playing the role of both father and mother: "As father he is a failure, but as a mother he is a success" (122).

The failure of the father lies in the fact that he shamefully gives in to the younger son's request for his inheritance. Worse than this "failure," however, is the shame the son brings upon the family. In an honour/shame society, the prodigal son brings shame upon himself because he essentially treats his father as if he were dead, when he asks to cash in his part of the family estate. He then wastes it and ends up starving in a foreign land, where he serves a Gentile farmer by feeding pigs, another shameful act for a Jew. Then he shames himself even further by envying the pigs for their food, which he cannot have.

He realizes that his father's servants eat better than he does, and that he can beg forgiveness and offer to work as a hired hand on his father's estate. So he practises saying the right words as he heads back home.

When the father sees him coming, he runs to his son – a shameful act in that society, since elder men did not run. The father kisses him, puts a robe on him, and tells the servants to "kill the fatted calf" for a celebration. The son begins to recite the words he has practised, but the father overwhelms him and prevents the completion of the well-rehearsed confession. He even places a ring on the son's finger, restoring him to his former rank as son.

Does the son then get a new inheritance? Does he return also to his mother? What happens to him next? We are left hanging, because the parable shifts at this point to the story of the older brother.

Many people leave the older brother out when they retell the story. Even the traditional name of the parable, The Prodigal Son, leaves out the older brother. But the story is about *two* sons and their father. And the older son has a good case against both his father and his younger brother by the social rules of the day.

The older son has followed the rules, supported the family and respected the father, but now he sees his younger brother shaming the family and getting rewarded for it. So he refuses to enter the party. Again the father comes out, this time to meet his older son, and to invite him to the celebration. The father even makes him a promise, saying, "all that is mine is yours" (v. 32). But again we are left hanging, because we do not learn whether or not the older son goes to the party, or what becomes of the relationship between the sons, the father, or the mother.

A traditional allegorical interpretation of this parable – rejected by scholars for the past 100 years – equates the older son with a Jewish legalist who strictly follows the law. God, represented by the father, favours the younger son, who is equated with a Christian. Favouring the younger son was not unusual in the Hebrew tradition – one needs only to recall the story of Jacob and Esau, and the preference given to Joseph over his older brothers, even though the law of primogeniture required favouring the older son. The point in this biased allegorical interpretation is that Christians are graced with this forgiveness while law-abiding Jews are caught in an old punishment-and-reward system. It's long past time we reject such allegorical anti-Semitism.

As already mentioned, we need to approach the parable from within the social world of first-century Palestine, which was honour/shame based. In his book *The God of Jesus*, Stephen Patterson concludes his honour/shame analysis of this parable with the notion that the Empire of God does not operate according to the rules of an honour/shame society, but rather on the basis of love, care, and reconciliation. *This* is "the basis for real life together" (158). I find Patterson's interpretation convincing.

Bernard Brandon Scott points out that both sons are chosen and rewarded:

The father is interested neither in morality nor in inheritance. He is concerned with the unity of his sons... The father does not reject. The metaphor for the Kingdom is the father's coming out, both for the younger son and for the elder. Apart from him is division and failure... (125)

In the parable, the fate of this family, which we might anachronistically call "dysfunctional," is left hanging. We never know what finally happens to them. But we do know that there *are* children who squander their parent's property and who cause enormous wreckage in their wake. Yet Jesus taught that even the worst behaviour can be forgiven if true repentance happens. Though the father and son would be shamed by the rules of the honour/shame society, Jesus teaches the different rules of God's Empire.

Questions for Discussion

1. *When have you ever experienced this kind of forgiveness in your life? Did you experience that forgiveness as coming from God, or from another person, or both?*
2. *Have there been times when you have felt like the elder brother?*
3. *Do you think the prodigal son really repents? Why?*
4. *Imagine that you are the mother in this family. How do you think you would have responded?*
5. *Have you experienced the kind of sibling rivalry described in this parable? What did it feel like to you?*

~ 12 ~

The Dishonest Manager

WHAT DO YOU THINK?
Can the whole economic system make us personally dishonest?

Luke 16:1–9

[1]Then Jesus said to the disciples, "There was a rich man who had a manager, and charges were brought to him that this man was squandering his property. [2]So he summoned him and said to him, 'What is this that I hear about you? Give me an account of your management, because you cannot be my manager any longer.' [3]Then the manager said to himself, 'What will I do, now that my master is taking the position away from me? I am not strong enough to dig, and I am ashamed to beg. [4]I have decided what to do so that, when I am dismissed as manager, people may welcome me into their homes.' [5]So, summoning his master's debtors one by one, he asked the first, 'How much do you owe my master?' [6]He answered, 'A hundred jugs of olive oil.' He said to him, 'Take your bill, sit down quickly, and make it fifty.' [7]Then he asked another, 'And how much do you owe?' He replied, 'A hundred containers of wheat.' He said to him, 'Take your bill and make it eighty.' [8]And his master commended the dishonest manager because he had acted shrewdly; for the children of this age are more shrewd in dealing with their own generation than are the children of light. [9]And I tell you, make friends for yourselves by means of dishonest wealth so that when it is gone, they may welcome you into the eternal homes."

A New Image

The challenge of understanding the meaning of this parable has kept interpreters busy for centuries. For an artist to represent this parable visually, without words, is even more challenging. Where is the focus of events in the parable: the firing, the choice of begging or digging, the idea of cutting the debts, or the commendation? All of these events are central to the story. How can we visualize them in four images?

The soliloquy (Luke's special tool) suggests that the story goes on in the manager's head. So a series of four reliefs of the manager's head, hands, and face, can communicate the events. The first image expresses his shock at being fired.

The second shows his dismay at his only apparent options of digging or begging.

The third, a brightened face and hand, shows his pleasure at the idea of reducing the debt so that he will be welcomed into the debtors' homes.

And in the fourth, his face shows the smug delight at the success of his scheming.

But how can the landlord, the digging/begging, and the debtors be represented visually? To do this, I have created small figures above the manager's head. The owner fires him in the first image.

He stands pointing a finger at the manager, ushering him off the estate because the owner has gotten reports of his initial mismanagement. Then, in the last image, the owner blesses him for his shrewdness.

The digging/begging options are also visualized above the manager's head, as he mulls his fate in the second panel.

The debtors are shown rewriting and reducing their contracted debts, as the manager brightens up with this shrewd idea.

The four relief sculptures are actually done on only two slabs of clay, which are interlocking and two-sided. The first side of the two slabs depict the firing and the mulling-of-options images. The second side of the two slabs depict the bright idea and the commendation.

In an economic system in which peasants were exploited by absentee landlords who employed corrupt managers, there were no good alternatives within that system for those without power or status. The alternatives for these people lay outside the system, that is, in exposing such corruption, and in preaching a totally different system, where such dishonesty would neither be practised nor rewarded. Jesus exposes the corruption and challenges us to create a different system – one that looks more like the Empire of God.

Parable Research

This parable, which is found only in Luke, has puzzled the church and biblical interpreters from the very beginning, because the manager is commended for cheating.

In the parable, the manager of a large estate is fired because the landlord hears he has mismanaged it. Making no excuses, he begins to worry about what he will do without this job. He rules out working as a day labourer, and begging as beneath him. Then he thinks of a plan to reduce the debts owed the landlord. He quickly gets the debtors to rewrite their contracts for lower amounts. For this shrewd behaviour, he is strangely commended by the landlord. In other words, he cheats and gets rewarded for it. What could this possibly mean?

There are almost as many different interpretations of this parable as there are interpreters. The first interpretation comes from Luke himself. After the much-debated verse 8a, where the commendation occurs, we find a number of sayings and moral applications. Scholars agree that these were added by Luke to Jesus' parable.

There are also some other things scholars agree upon. Assuming the tale is lifelike and not totally fanciful, the owner of the land was rich and probably an absentee landlord. This set him up as a villain in the eyes of the Galilean peasants in Jesus' audience, though he was likely *not* a villain for the authorities, who were busy monitoring Jesus' activities as he preached and travelled toward Jerusalem.

The manager was a common middle man between the landowner and the peasants and merchants. He, no doubt, added his "take" onto the amounts he was supposed to collect from the debtors and then pay to the owner. He would not have been a slave (even though slaves were sometimes managers) because the owner would not have fired a slave. Slaves were bought and sold, and would have been a saleable asset to the landowner. However, the threat of unemployment presented an even more dire situation to the manager than if he had been a slave, for he was too weak for digging and would likely have had to beg even though he was too proud for that. William Herzog stresses this vulnerability by saying that, either way, the manager's firing was a "death sentence" (*Subversive Speech*, 242).

It is most likely that the two debts mentioned, for oil and for wheat, were owed by merchants, not peasants, because the amounts were huge. Estimates vary from 1,100 to 1,000 bushels of grain, and from 500 to 1,000 gallons of olive oil. These very large amounts validate the observation that the owner was very well-off. It would require a large estate with fields for grain and orchards for olives to produce these quantities. Peasants would not have been able to incur such debts, let alone pay them. In addition, peasants could rarely read or write, so when the manager tells the debtors to write the 50 and 20 percent reductions in their debts, he is obviously speaking to merchants.

The shrewdness of the manager is emphasized in the way he cuts down their debts. First, he calls for each debtor to rewrite their contract, presumably before they can discover that he no longer has the authority to negotiate the debt, because he is now unemployed. Note also that he cuts his deals with each debtor separately, so they have no chance to compare notes on what is happening.

The general agreement of scholars seems to end at this point. There is no agreement on where the parable itself ends. The main debate centres on whether the parable ends *before* the commendation, or *after* it. If it ends at verse 7 (Crossan, *In Parables*, 109–110), we can ignore the unlikely instance of a rich, absentee landlord praising a manager who has cheated him. Also, it puts the saying (vs. 8b–9) out of the parable and thus into a commentary on the parable itself.

There is more agreement in modern scholarship that the parable ends after verse 8a, and includes the commendation for dishonestly/shrewdness; and that the owner is the one issuing this unlikely commendation. However, the commendation could also have been given by Jesus, because the Greek title *kyrios* can be translated as "Lord" (perhaps meaning Jesus), or as "master" (meaning the landlord). This ambiguity in the text has fuelled debate throughout Christian history.

As for how this parable can be interpreted or applied, it is most inviting to agree with C. H. Dodd, when he says there is "no certain clue to its application" (18). However, remaining clueless is not a comfortable position for experts to be in. Perhaps that's why Dodd goes on to speculate that Jesus may have been aiming the parable at the religious authorities who, like the manager, feathered their nests with dishonest dealings (18). One could go on to speculate that the owner is a symbol for God, who entrusts creation to such religious leaders, who in turn cheat on God but are forgiven for it when they, like the manager, "think strenuously and act boldly" (18).

Bernard Brandon Scott has a complex interpretation in his study of the social expectations and the most likely response of the audience to the parable. He notes how the peasant audience would have had sympathy for the manager, for he has no chance to defend himself before getting fired; and how they would have enjoyed the manager's rogue behaviour, his "getting even" with the despotic, rich landlord. Yet this "comedy" has a "barbed" ending, and the hearer is left uncomfortable for having sympathy for an immoral act. Scott concludes that this barb forces us, the readers of this parable, to "establish new coordinates for power, justice, and vulnerability. The kingdom is for the vulnerable, for masters and stewards [managers] who do not get even" (266).

This interpretation attracts me, because it makes God's Empire one of entirely different values, where power does not rest with land ownership or dishonest behaviour. In this interpretation, vulnerability is prized and "new coordinates" are required, themes very much in keeping with the actions and preaching of Jesus.

William Herzog's more political view furthers this line of interpretation. He points out that the manager is in the "retainer" class in this patron/client social structure, and that it is not just this retainer/manager who is corrupt, but the whole economic/political structure. In such a structure, the retainer/ manager used the "weapons of the weak," such as the reduction of the debt, in order to remind the landlord of his value as a skilled manager. That value also includes the manager's job of taking the fall for the landlord's usury – usury that was condemned in the Torah. Herzog goes on to point out that the landlord can easily make up the loss in income, which would have been large to the merchants or peasants, but relatively small in terms of his own overall wealth. He also gains public relations points with the merchants, because they will perceive *him*, not the manager, as the one ultimately responsible for lowering their debts. As a result, they will owe him favours. This may not be a parable of the reign of God," says Herzog, "but it suggests how the weapons of the weak can produce results in a world dominated by the strong" (*Subversive Speech*, 258).

I think it is reasonable to conclude that this parable is about a corrupt economic system. Jesus unmasks it and reveals its inner workings in order to promote its opposite, God's Empire, where all have enough and where there is no cheating or amassing of excessive wealth at the expense of poor.

Questions for Discussion

1. *After reading everything above, are you inclined to separate Luke's interpretation from Jesus' intention? Why?*
2. *What would you do in the manager's position?*
3. *What would you do in the landlord's position?*
4. *Do you think Jesus is commending dishonesty?*
5. *As you interpret this parable, where do you think God's Empire comes in?*

~ 13 ~

The Rich Man and Lazarus

WHAT DO YOU THINK?
What truths about wealth can we hear from the dead,
and how can we hear them?

Luke 16:19–31

19"There was a rich man who was dressed in purple and fine linen and who feasted sumptuously every day. 20And at his gate lay a poor man named Lazarus, covered with sores, 21who longed to satisfy his hunger with what fell from the rich man's table; even the dogs would come and lick his sores. 22The poor man died and was carried away by the angels to be with Abraham. The rich man also died and was buried. 23In Hades, where he was being tormented, he looked up and saw Abraham far away with Lazarus by his side. 24He called out, 'Father Abraham, have mercy on me, and send Lazarus to dip the tip of his finger in water and cool my tongue; for I am in agony in these flames.' 25But Abraham said, 'Child, remember that during your lifetime you received your good things, and Lazarus in like manner evil things; but now he is comforted here, and you are in agony. 26Besides all this, between you and us a great chasm has been fixed, so that those who might want to pass from here to you cannot do so, and no one can cross from there to us.' 27He said, 'Then, father, I beg you to send him to my father's house – 28for I have five brothers – that he may warn them, so that they will not also come into this place of torment.' 29Abraham replied, 'They have Moses and the prophets; they should listen to them.' 30He said, 'No, father Abraham; but if someone goes to them from the dead, they will repent.' 31He said to him, 'If they do not listen to Moses and the prophets, neither will they be convinced even if someone rises from the dead.'"

A New Image

Aclay image of the verbal images in this parable must do a number of things, one of which is show the extreme contrast between Lazarus and the rich man. It must also show the balanced parallelism of their conditions. In the sculpture I have created, the two men recline, one at ease, finely dressed, dining and enjoying his wealth, which is shown by a bag of money in one hand and a wine goblet in the other.

Lazarus, in contrast, is in the same reclining position, but reversed. *He* is reclining because he is sick, so sick he cannot avoid a dog licking his sores. His reversed but identical posture connects him with the rich man, yet he doesn't dine, enjoy wealth, or wear much clothing. He groans in his misery just as the rich man smiles proudly in his comfort.

A second set of images in relief represents the afterlife, in which Lazarus and the rich man have reversed roles. Lazarus rests in the bosom of Abraham; the rich man suffers in Hades and begs for a drop of water on his tongue. A gap divides them, although the two can talk across the chasm. I have depicted Abraham as a wise sage, who has compassion for both, even calling the rich man "child."

Abraham embraces Lazarus with one hand and advises the rich man with the other. Abraham declares that the rich man's privileges are gone now and no one can cross the great chasm. The afterlife is not changeable.

However, I believe the point of this tale is that *life* is changeable – *if* we heed the call to God's Empire from Abraham, Moses, the prophets, and Jesus.

Parable Research

The Rich Man and Lazarus parable, also called the "Rich Man, Poor Man," is a most vivid image of the radical reversal of life in the afterlife. In life, the rich man has it all – plenty of food and royal attire. So he pays no heed to Lazarus, who is dumped at his gate, near death, as the dogs wait to eat what is left of him. But in the afterlife, Lazarus has the honour of father Abraham's embrace, while the rich man is tormented in Hades. Truly, the reversal of their fortunes could not be more extreme.

Scholars disagree on whether this parable originated with Jesus, or with Luke, or with neither, or whether Luke and Jesus each contributed some parts to it.

One of the differences between this parable and the other parables is that it uses proper names: Abraham, and Lazarus (not to be confused with the brother of Mary and Martha, in John 11:1–2). This parable, with the Last Judgement, is also the only one that deals with the afterlife. Rudolph Bultmann holds, therefore, that the parable is "probably not a part of the preaching of Jesus" (*Jesus*, 104).

There is a division in the parable between verses 19–26, and verses 27–31. John Dominic Crossan thinks that the second part of the afterlife conversation sounds too much like the early church preaching after the Resurrection to have been authored by Jesus. But Crossan affirms that the early section is "an actual parable of Jesus" (*In Parables*, 68). Other scholars – such as Charles Hedrick and Norman Perrin, among others – simply do not consider this parable at all.

William Herzog, on the other hand, leans far to the side of Jesus' full authorship and considers the whole parable to be a fine example of "Jesus' pastoral parable on the Palestinian economy" (*Subversive Speech*, 128). It represents, says Herzog, Jesus' way of unmasking the unjust suppression of the poor and the conspicuous consumption of the rich. For Herzog, the parable is a unified whole that lays out a "social script" for the corruption of an urban elite and the disparately poor in an advanced agrarian society.

Scholars agree on the basic aspects of the parable:

- It only appears in Luke.
- The name *Lazarus*, which is unique, translates as "helped by God."
- The Vulgate used the name Dives for the rich man, but all agree that name is not in the original texts.
- *Hades* (Greek) is not the same as hell and is more like *Sheol* (Hebrew), an afterlife location where all go before the final separation of the righteous from the unrighteous.
- Similar afterlife reversals exist in Egyptian, Greek, and Jewish traditions, which Luke and/or Jesus could have used to create this parable.

The parable is addressed to the Pharisees, who Luke says "are lovers of money" (v. 14). However, the Pharisees were neither rich nor conspicuously consumptive, as were the Sadducees. A. T. Cadoux claimed this parable was Jesus' answer to the Pharisees, who asked Jesus for a sign to prove his message (124–126). Archibald Hunter believes that the rich man symbolized the Sadducees (83–84), and directly asserts that the parable was aimed at the Sadducees and was Jesus' rejection of *their* demand for a sign. Most agree that the parable does not condemn riches as such. Abraham himself was a rich man, as well as a model of hospitality. It was the whole economic system that was the problem.

Yet most commentators ignore these political issues and stress instead the personal issues of blindness, indifference, and insensitivity, which often come with riches. But Herzog says this is not the point. The rich man is rich because of the systemic oppression of the poor, and Lazarus is blessed and saved because of his poverty and suffering, not because of his piety, which is never mentioned.

Most scholars agree on the direct parallel in the reversal. For example, the earthly gate becomes a chasm in the afterlife. Lazarus begs for crumbs, and then later the rich man begs for a drop of water. In this life, the rich are protected by the economic system while in the next life the poor are protected by Abraham. The rich man is covered with fine clothes; Lazarus is covered with sores. Dogs attend him in this life, angels in the next. Those angels carry Lazarus away to Abraham, as compared to the rich man's burial. The implication is that Lazarus had no burial, the final insult on earth.

Herzog gives a vivid, though embellished, picture of the two men's condition:

Three items identify the rich man (*plousiōs*) as a member of the elite. He was "clothed in purple," the most expensive dye in the ancient world. Only the richest of the rich could afford it. He wears linen most likely imported from Egypt, and he serves great feasts, not just on special occasions but every day. He isolates and protects himself from the grim realities of the world by constructing a great ornamental gate that shuts out the world around him (*Prophet,* 121).

Of course, we do not know if the gate was "great" or "ornamental," but Herzog is making a point about the extreme conditions. He also conjectures how Lazarus may have arrived at the rich man's gate.

Lazarus is the poorest of the poor. He is a destitute beggar (*ptochos*) who has been "thrown down" at the rich man's gate. How did a beggar like Lazarus come into such desperate straits?... [when a son consumed more than he produced, he was] turned loose on the streets to become [a day laborer]... Day laborers lived just at or below the threshold of survival, dying slowly from the complications of malnutrition... This left begging as his last resort, but begging left one more destitute than working as a day laborer...too weak to move...full of sores, licked by street dogs, longing to eat even table scraps (*Prophet,*121).

In the afterlife, the reversal is clear, although Lazarus continues to be passive (Scott, 153) and silent, and the rich man continues to talk and assume his privileged attitude even while in torment. For example, he still does not speak to Lazarus, but directs Abraham to send Lazarus with a drop of water to cool his tongue, as if Lazarus were his servant. Abraham declares the request impossible, for a great chasm is fixed between them and cannot be crossed. Failing in his command, he begs for Lazarus to be sent to warn his five brothers on earth to avoid his fate in Hades. Abraham replies that they can listen to Moses and the prophets, who carry the same message. The rich man continues, unrepentant, to argue that they would repent if someone from the dead told them. Finally, Abraham rejects this argument too.

The debate continues on how we apply this parable. Although the rich man's brothers do not hear from the dead, *we* hear from the dead in this parable. Just as Thornton Wilder has Emily return from the dead in *Our Town*, and Charles Dickens has Ebenezer Scrooge visit his afterlife in *A Christmas Carol*, *we* have this parable to warn us. Do we respond to the poor Lazaruses in our midst with charity (scraps from our table), or do we seek to change the economic conditions that set up these extremes of rich and poor?

Do we take this parable as a moral example? Most scholars deny such an interpretation, because wealth as such is not condemned in the parable, and there is no evil behaviour assigned to the rich man other than ignoring Lazarus.

Is the parable an argument by Jesus that there is no need for signs, for the law and the prophets are enough? In this regard, Herzog adds a telling argument about the interpretation of the phrase "the poor you always have with you" (Mark 14:7, Matthew 26:11). This phrase has been used endlessly to excuse the abuse of the poor. But it means to say, rather, that when we see the poor Lazaruses in our streets, we have them (like a returned Lazarus, or Moses, or the prophets) to warn us of the fate of the rich man.

Other scholars stress the inability of the rich man to see Lazarus as his brother, even though they both have Abraham as their common father. Not only does the rich man not repent, he cannot see Lazarus as his kin (Herzog adds "class"). Bernard Brandon Scott takes a different course, saying, "Grace is the gate" that unites the rich and the poor (159).

When we seek to apply this parable, we seem to be warned against both the personal flaws of blindness, insensitivity, and indifference; and the public corruption of economic structures that exploit the poor for the benefit of the rich.

Different scholars lean in various directions. I appreciate William Herzog's economic/political system perspective, in spite of the embellishments he makes when describing the state of Lazarus and the rich man. For me, it is hard to ignore Jesus' overall message of concern for the poor, especially with the extra focus Luke gives to it. The poor rarely become poor by choice or by fate. Someone decides to horde the wealth, which keeps them poor; and we "always have the poor" with us because of these decisions. How could Jesus be ignorant of the systemic causes of such injustice?

Questions for Discussion

1. *Do you think Herzog is correct in stressing the economic conditions of Jesus' time? Why? Why not?*
2. *How do you interpret the message "the poor we always have with us"?*
3. *Is the problem the rich man's blindness, insensitivity, and indifference; or is it the whole economic system, or both? Why?*
4. *What can we do to help correct unjust economic systems?*

~ 14 ~

The Corrupt Judge

WHAT DO YOU THINK?
What can we do when officials such as judges take bribes?

Luke 18:1–8

[1]Then Jesus told them a parable about their need to pray always and not to lose heart. [2]He said, "In a certain city there was a judge who neither feared God nor had respect for people. [3]In that city there was a widow who kept coming to him and saying, 'Grant me justice against my opponent.' [4]For a while he refused; but later he said to himself, 'Though I have no fear of God and no respect for anyone, [5]yet because this widow keeps bothering me, I will grant her justice, so that she may not wear me out by continually coming.'" [6]And the Lord said, "Listen to what the unjust judge says. [7]And will not God grant justice to his chosen ones who cry to him day and night? Will he delay long in helping them? [8]I tell you, he will quickly grant justice to them. And yet, when the Son of Man comes, will he find faith on earth?"

A New Image

An image of this parable needs to express the comical corruption of this judge, who "neither fears God nor respects anyone." It also needs to show the persistence of the widow, whose courage exposes that corruption. There are two scenes: the widow demanding justice, and the judge finally relenting. So a two-sided sculpture works well. The front side shows the arrogant judge in a judge's wig high above the pleading widow, hiding his corruption behind the judicial bench.

That bench is called a Torah Court, and deals with money issues. The bench is ironically inscribed with a Torah and with the Hebrew word for justice/righteousness, *sedeca*. The judge is pointing to his left hand, miming the demand for a bribe. The widow cries out for her just due.

On the back side of the sculpture, her persistence successfully reveals his greatest vulnerability. His corruption of justice is literally exposed by his uncovered back side.

So exposed, his only power is shown to be the corrupted bench and the piles of money from the bribes, which hold him up. The Torah itself lies on the ground, crumpled by his corruption.

The heroic widow has found power in her powerlessness. Righteousness and justice prevail, because she demonstrates what the Torah demands and what Jesus lived out. The arrogant abuse of power is shown in its true nakedness, defeated by the non-violent exercise of courage by the poor widow.

Parable Research

This parable is a shocking and humorous story of corruption and persistence in which a judge who was supposed to be the godly protector of widows (Psalm 68:5) refused to protect this widow, and blatantly demonstrates that he neither "fears God nor respects anybody" (vv. 2,4).

For her part, the widow does the equally shocking (though not humorous) thing of going to his court and demanding justice. Women generally played no public role in Jesus' time, and a widow could be represented only by a male relative in public. Her daring act of confronting the judge was beyond the pale. Perhaps Jesus or Luke created this parable to shock their audience into listening to and remembering it.

The widow persists in her demand for justice, which probably would mean receiving her inheritance or dowry, or at least her maintenance from her dead husband's estate. (Maybe another relative, her "opponent," was seeking the inheritance.) The judge finally gives in, fearing her persistence will wear him down. Or maybe he just wants to be rid of her. In any event, justice prevails only because of her very unusual courage and persistence.

Luke is the only gospel writer to report this parable, so there is no way to see how he might have shaped it based on a comparison to another version. But there are numerous other signs of Luke's interpretation of it. Most evident is Luke's frequent focus on prayer, by which he also interprets the Friend at Midnight parable. Most commentators conclude that the idea of constantly pleading to God with prayerful requests sounds more like Luke and less like Jesus. David Buttrick finds that "banging on the doors of heaven...is hardly an appropriate theology of prayer" (186). Barbara Reid calls the idea of wearing God down in prayer "theologically abhorrent" (*Luke, Year C,* 234). Yet others, such as Arland Hultgren, say that this parable "is surely about prayer" (258).

Many scholars, however, agree that the parable itself (vv. 2–5) is probably from Jesus and that Luke surrounds it with verses 1, 6, 7, and 8, in order to take the edge off the shocking roles of the judge and the widow, and to interpret it as a call to persistent prayer.

Luke locates this parable just before another prayer-themed parable, that of the Pharisee and the Tax Collector. Both parables come at the close of the travel narrative in his end-time section, no doubt to address one of his other areas of concern – how to cope with the delayed second coming of Jesus. Luke likely sees the parable as encouraging the early, struggling Christian community with assurances that God will not delay long in providing justice, which would free them from oppression. When the "Son of Man" returns, he will expect faith on earth: for Luke, most likely evidenced by prayer. In other words, Luke is saying to his audience, "Hang on and pray persistently, like the widow persisted before the judge."

Barbara Reid notes that the use of the third person "he told" in verse 1 is a sign of Luke's hand. Also, "the Lord" is a post-resurrection name for Jesus, not one Jesus would have used of himself, yet more evidence of Luke's editing (228–229).

What, then, is the parable itself about if we look behind Luke's interpretation? Here we find more agreements and disagreements among interpreters. Most agree that the actions by the judge and the widow are extreme, and scholars often quote 2 Chronicles 19:6–7 on the expected behaviour of judges. In this passage, Jehoshaphat instructs them to rule,

> …on the Lord's behalf; he is with you in giving judgement. Now, let the fear of the Lord be upon you; take care what you do, for there is no perversion of justice with the Lord our God, or partiality, or taking of bribes.

The stakes get higher in Deuteronomy 27:19, where a curse is laid on those who deprive the alien, the orphan, or the widow of justice. Clearly, the judge in this parable is corrupt, not only for ignoring the pleas of a widow who should be given special protection, but for not fearing God, not respecting people, and for perverting justice and impartiality. Some interpreters assume that he is taking a bribe from the widow's opponent and could be holding out for a better one from her. This is not in the text, of course, but it is not a farfetched assumption either. His disregard for all the qualities that give honour to judges would have been considered shameful by Jesus' audience. Bernard Brandon Scott rules him to be an "outlaw judge" (180).

The powerless widow is apparently without any male relatives to plead her case. So she dares to enter the forbidden public realm of men to do the impossible – challenge a man of great power. However, she has the power of courage and persistence on her side, and she is "continually coming" to plead her case for justice. The alternative to getting justice in her case is most likely homelessness and even possible starvation. For without a male sponsor, she has few respectable means to support herself. Desperation is no doubt her motive, but she has the Torah on her side. The judge is *required* to protect her, even if he does not do so in fact.

There is much discussion about the judge's motive. According to the text, the judge says that the widow is "bothering me" and will "wear me out." John Donahue, quoting Kenneth Bailey, says that "bother" is too weak a translation (183). He prefers "work me over." Also, "wear me out" is too mild. The Greek word *hypopiazo* literally means "strike under the eye," and is often translated "give me a black eye." Some speculate that the judge's fear of a social "black eye" or of public embarrassment is his motive for responding to the widow. Yet Donahue makes a logical inference that the judge clearly cares nothing about his honour, which in that culture would have been based on fear of God and respect for others – virtues he rejects.

That the judge would literally fear the widow's physical violence is most unlikely. There is no evidence of a physical threat beyond this Lukan soliloquy of the judge, and it is often seen as humorous. Why would a powerful judge fear the fists of a poor widow in a public court? However, the humour is too often turned against the widow, suggesting that "he is tired of her perpetual nagging and wants to be left in peace" (Jeremias, 115). In this interpretation, the widow is dismissed as a nag instead of one who is truly heroic. She has the courage to speak truth to power and to demand justice, and she does so without violence. Those actions, as we have seen throughout the gospels, represent the way of Jesus.

To be sure, there is humour in this story. The judge is so unlikely as to be a cartoon figure, and his behaviour is villainously absurd. So the joke is on him, not her. The widow is the model of what Jesus himself taught and demonstrated – justice without violence.

Questions for Discussion

1. *The interpretation that sees the meaning of the parable to be justice instead of prayer is debatable, especially because Luke favours the latter. What do you think?*
2. *Some have seen the judge as a God figure because he finally grants the widow's plea. What do you think: is he a God figure or an arrogant buffoon? Or something else?*
3. *The widow has been seen as a nag. How would you describe her?*
4. *Was justice done, or should the widow have shut up and left him in peace?*

~ 15 ~

The Pharisee and the Tax Collector

WHAT DO YOU THINK?
Why do colonized people fight each other?

Luke 18:9–14

[9]He also told this parable to some who trusted in themselves that they were righteous and regarded others with contempt: [10]"Two men went up to the temple to pray, one a Pharisee and the other a tax collector. [11]The Pharisee, standing by himself, was praying thus, 'God, I thank you that I am not like other people: thieves, rogues, adulterers, or even like this tax collector. [12]I fast twice a week; I give a tenth of all my income.' [13]But the tax collector, standing far off, would not even look up to heaven, but was beating his breast and saying, 'God, be merciful to me, a sinner!' [14]I tell you, this man went down to his home justified rather than the other; for all who exalt themselves will be humbled, but all who humble themselves will be exalted."

A New Image

A visual image of this parable needs to account for the economic and political context of the Temple. Both the Pharisee and the tax collector were locked into this system of tithes and taxes. Both tithing and taxes were part of what held up the Temple system, so I have imbedded the two characters in the pillars of my sculpture. The Temple was supposed to be where God could be heard and responded to in prayer, but it had been corrupted by the whole system of Roman occupation, which demanded taxes to pay for the oppression it laid on the people. That corruption is represented in the frieze of my sculpted temple, by toga-wearing Roman aristocrats who enjoy the opulence these taxes provide them.

On side one of this two-sided sculpture, the Pharisee is piously praying, judging, and shaming the tax collector, even as the tax collector beats his chest, a gesture of extreme remorse. Both are dominated by their Roman overlords.

On the second side of the sculpture, the Pharisee is shocked to see that the tax collector, a "sinner" by occupation, is justified rather than himself, a righteous one by profession. The tax collector is dancing at the news that his burden of guilt is lifted.

But both the tax collector and the Pharisee are still imbedded in and oppressed by the temple pillars. The temple frieze still contains a Roman, who on this side of the sculpture is a mounted soldier charging to war, symbolizing the perpetual wars the people of occupied Palestine unwillingly support via the extortionist taxes they must pay.

Meanwhile, the whole structure of the temple is beginning to crack.

It seems that Jesus was not only talking about prayer, but also about the corruption of the Temple, which had become a "den of robbers" (Mark 11:17, Matthew 21:13, Luke 19:46).

Parable Research

This parable is frequently interpreted as a simple, clear-cut example of the right and wrong attitude for prayer. That is, the humility of the tax collector is good, and the pride of the Pharisee is bad. The message: be humble in prayer like the tax collector, and beg for mercy, also like the tax collector, instead of being proud of your piety, like the Pharisee who lists his virtues and who condemns others.

This is a tempting reading of the parable, and it is encouraged by the framing Luke apparently wraps around it. But if we look behind Luke's editing and include the economic and political context, the parable looks very different.

Scholars generally agree that this parable begins with verse 10 and that Luke inserts his bias in verse 9, when he says that Jesus told this parable to "some who trusted themselves and regarded others with contempt." This is typical of Luke's rejection of the Pharisees.

Scholars also see this parable as paired with the Corrupt Judge and Persistent Widow parable, which Luke also frames with his theology on how best to pray.

Many commentators warn modern readers against projecting too much judgement on the boasting Pharisee, because such recitation of one's piety (tithing and fasting) was common at the time of the parable. (Note how Paul occasionally boasts of his pious accomplishments in 2 Corinthians 11:16–33 and elsewhere.) There is enough in the parable, however, to caricature the pious Pharisee, who nevertheless would have been highly honoured – as opposed to his polar opposite, the tax collector, who would have been shamed and despised.

Having said that, if we include the economic and political context, we find some hidden commonalities between these two men. Here is where Jesus' shocking twists come in.

On the surface, the Pharisee would have been considered a model citizen and a very active lay leader in the community and religious body. (These two roles were inseparable in biblical times.) He not only practised what was preached, and observed the Torah, he claimed to have exceeded the tithes and fasting requirements. He sought to keep his daily life and the Temple pure, that is, free of unclean people and unholy deeds. Yet the tax collector dares to pray in the Temple, when even his presence there would have been forbidden. Arland Hultgren says Jesus' audience "would never have heard of a tax collector going to the temple to pray...a rather shocking spectacle" (121). Why? The tax collector was not your modern IRS bean counter. He was a low-level functionary under a chief tax collector, such as Zaccheaus (Luke 19:1–10). These chief tax collectors got rich on the gouging work of the lowly tax collectors, who collected the tributes that Rome demanded and enforced. The low-level tax collectors were front men who bore the shaming and hatred of the taxpayers, and were so despised that Jews were forbidden to do this work. The anger of the people towards them was justified in that such taxes went not to the common good for public benefit. Rather, these taxes went to help Rome continue its occupation, aristocratic pleasures, and conquests. Thus, the tax collectors were seen as traitors doing Rome's work of extracting money for its empire.

What commentators often overlook is that the Pharisee was part of a similar system of tax extraction, though these taxes didn't go directly to Rome, but to the urban elites who ruled through the Temple. As William Herzog puts it, the tithes rendered to the Temple supported the elite priestly families. "The common peasants," on the other hand, "lived in squalor while they paid their temple tribute to support the conspicuous consumption of urban elites in Jerusalem" (*Subversive Speech*, 179).

These tithes and other taxes were part of the exploitation system that placed the Pharisee and the tax collector on the same level. Far from being the ideal citizen/religious leader, the Pharisee was part of the system that kept the poor poor, by shaming sinners like the tax collector. In other words, his prayer of thanks that he is "not like other people: thieves, rogues, adulterers, or even like this tax collector" was deliberately meant to shame the tax collector and was one of the ways the system was maintained. Both men extract money the people need to survive, but only the tax collector begs for mercy from God. By contrast, the Pharisee brags about himself and condemns the obvious bad guy. The economic and political realities set up these obvious good guy/bad guy roles, even as both are doing essentially the same thing.

It may be a stretch to go as far as Herzog does to read Jesus using this parable as a way of unmasking and decoding the whole system of taxes and tithes. Herzog sees it as Jesus' "pedagogy of the oppressed…designed to enable peasants to demystify the temple… [To] name oppression as a prelude to renaming their world… [The parable provided] a model of a figure who refused to be silenced but found his voice in the process of discovering God" (193). Jesus names the tax collector as the one who went home justified. Clearly, more than a good prayer/bad prayer attitude is present here.

The last verse of the parable itself, "he went down to his home justified," is curious. Why is his "home" mentioned? The book *The Social World of Luke-Acts* (edited by Jerome Neyrey) contains a fascinating answer, in a chapter by John Elliott (211–240). Elliott shows how Luke moved the emerging Jesus movement from the Temple to the household.

> The Temple, at first the locale of hope for salvation and a symbol of Israel's holy union with God, eventually is unmasked as a political concentration of power opposed to God's people and the truly righteous. The household…once the gathering place of the powerless and the marginalized, eventually emerges as the institution where God's spirit is truly active" (217).

Elliot points out that by the time of Paul's evangelism, the Jesus movement was gathering in house churches. The Temple had been given up as the location of God's special presence, as it lay in ruins after 70 CE.

Was Jesus, as distinct from Luke, organizing this movement away from the Temple? That is a possibility suggested by the fact that the tax collector appeals directly to God and God's mercy without the intermediation of the Temple or of its high priests. Whatever the case, there is clearly more to this parable than a sermon on bad guys praying pridefully, and good guys praying humbly – the usual interpretation. It shows how and why the factionalism of oppressed groups works in a conquered and occupied land.

Questions for Discussion

1. *What do you think this parable is about?*
2. *Does the economic and political context make a difference to how you interpret the parable? If so, how? If not, why not?*
3. *Imagine yourself in the parable as a third visitor to the Temple. What would you be thinking and feeling as you observe the actions of the Pharisee and the tax collector?*
4. *Imagine that you are part of the audience listening to Jesus tell this parable. As a Pharisee, what do you think your reaction would have been? As a peasant, or as a tax collector or other outsider, what do think your reaction would have been?*
5. *Does the idea of Jesus trying to organize the peasants to rise up fit with your image of Jesus?*

Parables in
The Gospel of Mark

~ 16 ~

The Sower

WHAT DO YOU THINK?
Will perseverance succeed in bringing God's Empire of peace and justice?

¹Again he began to teach beside the sea. Such a very large crowd gathered around him that he got into a boat on the sea and sat there, while the whole crowd was beside the sea on the land. ²He began to teach them many things in parables, and in his teaching he said to them: ³"Listen! A sower went out to sow. ⁴And as he sowed, some seed fell on the path, and the birds came and ate it up. ⁵Other seed fell on rocky ground, where it did not have much soil, and it sprang up quickly, since it had no depth of soil. ⁶And when the sun rose, it was scorched; and since it had no root, it withered away. ⁷Other seed fell among thorns, and the thorns grew up and choked it, and it yielded no grain. ⁸Other seed fell into good soil and brought forth grain, growing up and increasing and yielding thirty and sixty and a hundredfold." ⁹And he said, "Let anyone with ears to hear listen!"

¹⁰When he was alone, those who were around him along with the twelve asked him about the parables. ¹¹And he said to them, "To you has been given the secret of the kingdom of God, but for those outside, everything comes in parables; ¹²in order that 'they may indeed look, but not perceive, and may indeed listen, but not understand; so that they may not turn again and be forgiven.'"

¹³And he said to them, "Do you not understand this parable? Then how will you understand all the parables? ¹⁴The sower sows the word. ¹⁵These are the ones on the path where the word is sown: when they hear, Satan immediately comes and takes away the word that is sown in them. ¹⁶And these are the ones sown on rocky ground: when they hear the word, they immediately receive it with joy. ¹⁷But they have no root, and endure only for a while; then, when trouble or persecution arises on account of the word, immediately they fall away. ¹⁸And others are those sown among the thorns: these are the ones who hear the word, ¹⁹but the cares of the world, and the lure of wealth, and the desire for other things come in and choke the word, and it yields nothing. ²⁰And these are the ones sown on the good soil: they hear the word and accept it and bear fruit, thirty and sixty and a hundredfold."

²¹He said to them, "Is a lamp brought in to be put under the bushel basket, or under the bed, and not on the lampstand? ²²For there is nothing hidden, except to be disclosed; nor is anything secret, except to come to light."

(See also Matthew 13:3–8, Luke 8:5–8, Thomas 9:1–5.)

A New Image

An image of the Sower has a lot to communicate. I see a very confident and proud sower in-the-round, spreading her seeds. A woman instead of a man provides an unusual image for a farmer, but it is truer to life in impoverished lands, where women often do much of the farming.

Behind her there follows a relief sculpture, which depicts a barren path, birds, rocks, thorns, and finally the great crop.

The sower stands erect and proud, because she is free from the need of self-protection and free for self-propagation in God's Empire.

She has nothing to defend because there is enough for all. In real life there are setbacks – barren paths, birds, stones, and thorns. However, in the end, a great crop grows. Her posture, gestures, and countenance have to communicate all of this. To be sure, it is unlikely that such a peasant would be so proud. But the message of Jesus is also very unlikely within the empires of this world. Yet amid all of our struggles, a great harvest and the great supper await.

Parable Research

Mark, Matthew, and Luke have tried to tell us why Jesus spoke in parables, as well as who can understand them and who cannot. They also show us how to go about interpreting the Sower parable, using allegory to do so. The critical question for us is, do we take the allegorical interpretation to be that of Jesus, or that of the synoptic gospel writers who wrote the parables down years after Jesus' execution? Is this Jesus speaking in the words that surround the parables (the frames), or are these frames the construction of the gospel writers? Most scholars since Adolf Jülicher distinguish Jesus' parable from the allegory of the synoptic gospels allegory, and conclude that the allegory does not belong to Jesus but is the early church's creation. We must untangle this issue before we get back to the parable itself and what Jesus might have meant by it.

There are three parts of this parable and the framing around it that make a critical claim on how we interpret it. The first part is the parable itself (vv. 3–9). The second part explains why Jesus spoke in parables generally (vv. 10–12). The third part is the allegorical interpretation of the Sower parable (vv.13–20). I will focus on Mark's version of The Sower, even though there are similar ones in Matthew, Luke, and Thomas. Thomas alone presents the parable with no interpretation.

Most scholars start with Mark on the assumption that Matthew and Luke depend on his version. (Bernard Brandon Scott's view is an exception. He believes Luke wrote his version independently.)

The second part of the text is the explanation of why Jesus spoke in parables. The answer Mark gives contradicts Jesus' other words and deeds (vv. 21–22 and throughout). Mark has Jesus say that he speaks to the crowds in parables so that they will *not* perceive or understand or be forgiven (v. 12). Jesus will explain the parable of the sower only to his inner circle of followers so they alone will understand.

C. H. Dodd believes that Jesus didn't need to explain why he spoke in parables at all, because parables were a common teaching method of the rabbis. In other words, the question would probably not even have been raised in Jesus' time (4). However, the question *was* raised by the early church and by the gospel writers, because they were puzzled by the parables. Mark, followed by Matthew and Luke, has Jesus say, "To you has been given the secret of the kingdom of God, but for those outside, everything comes in parables; in order that [to paraphrase Isaiah 6:9–10] 'they may indeed look but not perceive, and may indeed listen, but not understand; so that they may not turn again and be forgiven.'"

This claim of insiders getting the secret, straight story, and outsiders getting mystical, parabolic confusion, is called the "hardening theory" because it takes such a hard line against the outsiders who do not get it. The theory also questions the words that the synoptic writers put in Jesus' mouth, because they are so alien to the general inclusiveness of Jesus' whole mission.

Next, Mark's Jesus decodes the parable with an allegory (vv. 14–20), which John Donahue calls "the parade example of the use of allegory" (46).

Parables call for decisions and we certainly have a choice to make here. For instance, we can go along with the synoptic interpretation of the parable as an allegory of how the seeds (Jesus' words) are received. According to this interpretation, they are 1.) snatched by the birds/devil, 2.) wilted on rocks of persecution, 3.) choked by thorns of riches and material possessions, and 4.) sown on the good soil of willing hearers who "bear fruit thirty and sixty and a hundredfold." This has been by far the most common choice of interpretation made throughout the history of the church because, of course, this is what the synoptic gospels say.

The other choice is to follow the last 100 years of scholarly research most of which attempts to get behind the agenda of the gospel writers to Jesus' intent. Bernard Brandon Scott declares that we cannot reach back to Jesus' actual words, but we can reach his "originating structure," that is, Jesus' central idea in the parables.

There are convincing reasons to follow the scholarly research, the most telling of which is Mark's claim that Jesus sought to keep the meaning of the parables a secret to outsiders. Such secrecy conflicts with the otherwise dominant, inclusive message of Jesus. Indeed, Mark himself reports Jesus saying just the opposite of secrecy in the text immediately following his allegorical interpretation. Jesus says, in verses 21–22, that no one lights a lamp and puts it under a basket or a bed. The word, like the light, is to be seen, not hidden. Some scholars go further in this direction and claim that the parable itself was written or adapted by Mark to fit the allegory (Patterson, *The God of Jesus*, 132; Crossan *In Parables*, 41–42). In general, scholars agree that the fact that the parable circulated *without* this allegorical interpretation in Thomas proves that the interpretation was attached later by the writers of the synoptic gospels (Funk, *Five Gospels*, 56). "Further, the allegory does not match the parable and is inconsistent within itself: the seed first stands for the word, the gospel, then it represents different kinds of responses to the message" (56).

Other reasons stack up against the allegorical interpretation. For instance, the rocky ground of persecution was an early church concern, whereas Jesus' immediate adversaries were the scribes and the Pharisees, but not direct Roman persecution. Also, the words used in the allegory – such as "*logos*," the Word; and "preach"; and also the words "sow," "lure," and "root" – were common to the early church, but they were not used by Jesus (Donahue, 46).

A. T. Cadoux points out that the parables had "largely become unintelligible to the [early] Church" (25). So they made the parables fit their context, in this case by inverting the parable's emphasis on the successful seeds growing in good soil to an emphasis on the failure of the seeds sown in poor soil. Cadoux and others point out how confusing the allegory makes the parable itself. One example is that the seeds sown on the path and snatched by the birds (allegorically, the devil) would not have grown anyway on a trodden path. So it makes no sense to assume they would have grown on the path if the birds/devil were absent.

By contrast, Luise Schottroff rejects this separation of parable and allegory and reads the parable and Mark's application all together as a unit. She admits that the back and forth of the various seeds, soil, and human hearing present "disorder" (*Parables*, 71). But the "meaning is quite clear," she says, and "it does not make sense to speak of allegory here" (71). For Schottroff, the meaning of the whole passage, including both the parable and Mark's interpretation of it, is the hearing and doing of the Word of God. In other words, the *Shema Israel*, which is hearing and doing the Torah.

Though the *Shema* was a daily prayer, it was very difficult to live out under the conditions of Roman occupation in Mark's time (near or after the defeat of the Jews in the war of 66–70 CE). Just as seeds sown on rocky and thorny paths have difficulty growing, Jesus' followers are likewise tempted by persecution, greed, and Roman oppression not to hear and do God's will, the Torah. But for those who do, great abundance (a hundredfold harvest) awaits (77–78).

I need to mention one additional debate, which centres on the description of sowing *before* plowing. David Buttrick calls the sower a "dummy" for sowing seeds before plowing the ground (64). Joachim Jeremias, however, claims that this was a common practice in that day (9, footnote). Many reject Jeremias' claim though. The most telling argument against the sow-first-plow-second practice is that the seeds sown on the path and among rocks and thorns probably would not have failed to produce had the path, rocks, and thorns been plowed over *after* the sowing (Hulgren, 187). Having said that, Bernard Brandon Scott is probably right to say that this extended debate over which comes first, the sowing or the plowing, is probably "irrelevant" (353).

To summarize my thoughts thus far, while acknowledging Luise Schottroff's point about keeping the parable and Mark's application together, I still find Mark's exclusion inconsistent with Jesus' inclusiveness.

Having moved beyond the gospels' claim that the crowds were not meant to understand the parables, and beyond the allegorical interpretation of the parable, we can now ask what Jesus meant by the Sower parable.

John Dominic Crossan's summary is most convincing. According to him, the "miracle," "surprise," and "gift" of the hundredfold growth of the seeds planted on good soil is the main message of the parable (*In Parables*, 51). In the first century, growth of plants was not seen as a biological or organic process, but as a miracle of God, a holy gift. Thus, Jesus' message of God's saving Empire was like that miracle of seed growth. Even if the sower was a "dummy" to waste all that seed on the path, rocks, and thorns, Jesus' followers can take heart that the miracle will happen even when our preaching of God's presence with us seems to be wasted like such seeds. Virtually all modern interpreters see the hundredfold growth to be a magnificent harvest, except for Scott, who judges it to be a normally good crop. Barbara Reid calls it "astronomical," "unimaginable," and "explosive," an "inconceivable abundance" of God's graciousness (*Mark, Year B*, 96).

Reid offers four applications of this abundance: 1.) the profligate sowing suggests that all people are included in God's realm, 2.) the miracle of abundance offers encouragement to preachers who see few results from their preaching, 3.) the huge crop offers the hope of freedom for poor peasants, who could have purchased land with the extra profits that a huge harvest would provide, and 4.) the promise of abundance offers wisdom to lax congregations who stand as obstacles to preaching (102).

I would like to highlight Reid's third application, which offers hope for peasants from a huge harvest, but which seems an interpretive stretch in terms of the text itself. A less direct hope for such freedom is found in Cadoux, who says "[the parable's] central emphasis is on life that secures its survival by self-propagation rather than by self-protection" (155). Although this hope is less immediate than Reid's projection of peasant freedom, Cadoux's hope of the self-propagation of the seeds and, thus, of the self-reliance of peasants and of all people is a helpful application. Although some seeds (Jesus' words of hope for God's Empire) are lost, the great harvest makes up for all this initially futile effort, and then some.

The opposite of self-propagation is self-protection, which is the way of the powers of this world, in this case the Roman empire and its local collaborators, who lived by exploiting the poor and by protecting themselves with violence. The poor, the hungry, the peacemakers, those who mourn, and those who are persecuted – whom Jesus blesses in the Beatitudes (Matthew 5:1–12, Luke 6:20–23) – are like the seeds in good soil. They need not live their lives defensively protecting their possessions, which moth and rust corrupt. Rather, they can live by self-propagation, which suggests Gandhi's saying that there is enough for our needs, but not for our greed. The "enough" is the self-propagation of all we need in God's Empire, where all have enough for life.

Questions for Discussion

1. *Why is it important to question the gospel writers' statement that Jesus excluded the crowd from understanding? What is wrong with only a few insiders understanding the parables?*
2. *Could it be that Mark, Matthew, and Luke got it wrong, or were they only adapting the parable to their situation some generations after Jesus? In what ways do we do the same?*
3. *How would you interpret and apply the parable of the sower?*
4. *Did A. T. Cadoux's distinction between self-propagation and self-protection influence your interpretation of the parable? If so, how? If not, why not?*

~ 17 ~

The Seed and the Harvest

WHAT DO YOU THINK?
Which is the answer to violence: more swords or more plows?

Mark 4:26–29

[26]He also said, "The kingdom of God is as if someone would scatter seed on the ground, [27]and would sleep and rise night and day, and the seed would sprout and grow, he does not know how. [28]The earth produces of itself, first the stalk, then the head, then the full grain in the head. [29]But when the grain is ripe, at once he goes in with his sickle, because the harvest has come."

(See also Thomas 21:4.)

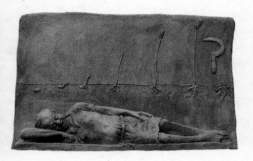

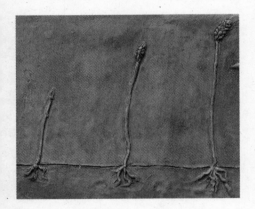

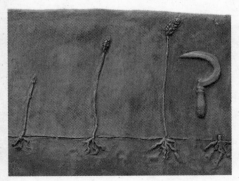

A New Image

The brevity of this parable and its seeming simplicity are deceiving. Before we can harvest its meaning, we must dig deep.

When I imagine this parable, I see a sleeping farmer. He is sleeping but behind him the seed grows and becomes a blade, then an ear...and finally a full grain on a relief tableau.

Then it is time for the harvest, a powerful symbol of God's just judgement.

Mark's phrase "goes in with his sickle" (v. 29), which describes the action of the farmer harvesting the grain, is particularly critical to the interpretation of this parable. The phrase itself is a recasting of a similar phrase from Joel's war scroll (3:9–14), where Joel reverses Isaiah's and Micah's "swords-to-plows" call for peace (Isaiah 2:04 and Micah 4:03). Instead, Joel calls for war, for "plows to swords" (3:10).

In other words, in terms of the biblical texts, to "go in with the sickle" can mean either a call to peaceful harvest, or a call to war. I have attempted to depict both possible meanings of this reference by sculpting an image of pounding plows into swords, and an image of pounding swords into plows.

My first image, which shows the call to war, depicts a man beating a plow into a sword over an anvil. I also wanted to show some of the results of war, so I have included an image of a woman and child, both victims of war.

The second image shows the call to peace. Here I show a man holding a sword over an anvil and a woman hammering it into a plow.

I have sculpted both the swords-to-plows image and the plows-to-swords image on the back side of the tableau of the seeds growing into the full grain.

Compared to other images of these Isaiah and Micah passages (such as the one at the United Nation's plaza of a man pounding a sword into a plow), the one I have created depicts a *group* effort, with a young woman initiating the pounding and an older man assisting.

This interpretation of the phrase to "go in with the sickle" and of the swords-to-plows imagery is consistent with Jesus' rejection of swords (war) in all four gospels: "all who take the sword will perish by the sword" (Matthew 26:52). Jesus seems to imply instead that those who live by the plow shall live.

The gracious mystery of growth in Mark's parable is experienced by all farmers and gardeners as seeds sprout and grow, we do "not know how" (v. 27). "Going in with the sickle" can mean either war or peace. It is up to *us* to reap the harvest of peace.

Parable Research

The parable of the seed and the harvest appears only in Mark, although there are faint parallels in the non-canonical Gospel of Thomas (21). Scholars question why Matthew and Luke did not adopt it, when they had already taken so much else from Mark.

The meaning of the parable has puzzled scholars as well. Not only do Luke and Matthew avoid it, so do some parable scholars, such as William Herzog. Others, such as Barbara Reid and John Donahue, give a number of optional interpretations.

The Seed and the Harvest parable is sandwiched between the Sower and the Mustard Seed parable, and Mark's interpretation of that parable. Mark saw Jesus comparing God's Empire to the mystery of natural growth. But what is that metaphorical connection exactly?

In this parable, the human contribution to the growth of the seeds is minimal. The farmer is involved with the growing plants only at the beginning and end of the growth process. He scatters seeds and then does nothing but sleep and rise until the grain is ripe. Some scholars read this as a lazy farmer who "does not know how" the crop grows. Meanwhile, the earth produces automatically. But growing "by itself" (the translation of the Greek *automate)* would not have been understood in Jesus' time as referring to mechanical or biological growth. Rather, the growth is by the grace of God alone. It clearly "alludes to divine activity" (Hultgren, 387).

The rhythm of growth moves from seed, to blade, to ear, to full grain (Donahue 34–36). In the parable, that rhythm, which is the rhythm of God's creation, is juxtaposed with the rhythm of the farmer's sleeping and rising, night and day. These two rhythms of God's time and human time intersect when the harvest is ready. Then the unknowing farmer wakes up and "goes in with his sickle."

As I suggested in my discussion of the sculpture, much is made of this phrase, "goes in with his sickle," which is adapted from Joel's war scroll, and which stands in such contrast to Micah's and Isaiah's call to "beat swords into plows and spears into pruning hooks." Joel's war scroll reads as follows:

Proclaim this among the nations:
Prepare war,
> stir up the warriors.
Let all the soldiers draw near,
> let them come up.
Beat your plowshares into swords,
> and your pruning hooks into spears,
> let the weakling say "I am a warrior..."
Put in the sickle,
> for the harvest is ripe.
Go in, tread,
> for the winepress is full.
The vats overflow,
> for their wickedness is great... (3:9–10, 13)

Is this parable, then, a call to war, much like when the Zealots appealed for a violent overthrow of Roman rule? Or is it a rejection of any human efforts to bring about God's Empire, which is often symbolized as a harvest? Clearly, the parable points to growth as God's doing and therefore seems to council patience. The harvest comes *automate*, automatically, without any of the farmer's effort.

Bernard Brandon Scott suggests that the hearer must decide if the parable is a sign of God's grace and peace in the present, or "the apocalyptic war motif of Joel" for the future. He opts for the God of grace and peace in the present. So perhaps the parable was meant to correct Joel's call to war. Jesus often said, "You have heard it said, but I say..."

Scott also points out that the farmer's inaction and the automatic growth indicate that the land is on sabbatical. The crop harvested is a sabbatical, "aftergrowth" crop. Whereas Joel reversed Isaiah's call to peace, Jesus, in turn, reverses Joel in this parable: "the harvest is no longer the apocalyptic war but a harvest of sabbatical aftergrowth planted by an ignorant farmer" (370). God's time is a time of peace.

1. *Why would Jesus' audience be impressed with the growth of seeds and plants?*
2. *Who do you think best gives voice to Jesus' perspective on war and peace: Joel or Isaiah?*
3. *What examples of "war scrolls" do we have today?*
4. *What examples of the call to peace, to beat swords into plows, do we have today?*

~ 18 ~

The Mustard Seed

WHAT DO YOU THINK?
What symbol best describes God's rule: a tiny seed or great tree?

³⁰He also said, "With what can we compare the kingdom of God, or what parable will we use for it? ³¹It is like a mustard seed, which, when sown upon the ground, is the smallest of all the seeds on earth; ³²yet when it is sown it grows up and becomes the greatest of all shrubs, and puts forth large branches, so that the birds of the air can make nests in its shade."

(See also Ezekiel 31:1–14, Matthew 13:31–32, Luke 13:19, Thomas 20:2.)

A New Image

There are two main scenes in the parable of the mustard seed, and this suggests a two-sided relief: the planting of the tiny seed on the one side, and the resulting mustard bush on the other.

On the first side, a woman bends over to plant the seed, a symbol of hope for God's Empire. A man mocks her hope with laughter. Another stands in worship of a great tree. A symbol of imperial might, the large tree speaks of military power and the hegemony of the Roman and Davidic empires, the complete opposite of the tiny mustard seed. Other nations come to these empires to pay tribute, like birds coming to nest in the branches of the tree.

On the second side of the relief, the tiny mustard seed has grown into a large bush able to shelter wildlife. The woman who planted the seed sings out joyfully at its growth, while the laughter of the mocker ends in dismay and wonder. The worshipper is confused by the end of the false hope of the military empire, which dies like the great tree with withered branches. While birds flock to the mustard bush and build nests there, a vulture of death and despair rests on the limp and withered limbs of this tree of death.

Parable Research

The parable of the mustard seed is often confused with Matthew 17:20 and Luke 17:06, in which Jesus says, "if you have faith the size of a mustard seed, you will say to this mountain [or tree, in Luke's version], 'Move from here to there,' and it will move…" This saying and the parable are not related, except in the sense that the small seed is a useful simile.

Using similes and metaphors is "indirect communication," as Søren Kierkegaard called it. Indirect communication is necessary in religion because spiritual realities are not physically visible and therefore are not subject to direct and precise language. We also use indirect language because we, as imperfect humans, have a way of blocking out the very wisdom we need for our spiritual well-being. So prophets come to us with indirect words.

In the Mustard Seed parable, Jesus built on the indirect communication in the sacred scriptures of his day, specifically the words of prophet Ezekiel, as C. H. Dodd and others have pointed out (153).

In Ezekiel 31:1–14, the prophet used indirect communication in the form of a simile to compare the pharaoh with a cedar of Lebanon. Instead of telling a story to engage his audience, as Jesus did in the parables, Ezekiel used gushing flattery. He trapped the pharaoh with nine verses of flattering praise. Ezekiel asks him, "Who are you like in your greatness?" Then he answers his own question by using a simile, which compares the pharaoh to "a cedar of Lebanon with fair branches and forest shade…its top among the clouds." Ezekiel entices the pharaoh to enjoy this flattery, and goes on to say that all the nations live under the pharaoh's shade tree like "the birds of the air that make nests in its boughs."

The simile seems innocuous, but when we translate those images into their imperial counterparts we see another reality altogether, in which other nations are like birds, subservient to the Egyptian empire, coming to pay tribute, losing sons and daughters to slavery, and allowing the pharaoh to stand tall and proud like a giant cedar tree.

Ezekiel goes on and on singing "Hail to the Chief" until verse 10, when he suddenly describes the pharaoh's defeat because of his pride and the wickedness of the land. The great tree of the pharaoh is cut down, the branches are broken, and the country is "handed over to death" (v. 14).

This tree simile in the Hebrew Bible is essential to understanding Jesus' use of this parable and other parables in general. Judea in Jesus' time was a conquered nation, an exploited colony of Rome. But Jews never lost their pride and their hope of a return to the Davidic empire which, like Pharaoh's Egypt and Caesar's Rome, dominated the nations around it, and which seemed safe and secure because of the military power it wielded in David's and Solomon's time. Thus, when Jesus spoke of the Empire of God, his listeners thought he meant this Davidic empire. The oppression of Roman rule would be overthrown, and Jews would be safe and secure again. For a while, they even thought Jesus was the new David.

So Jesus shocked his audience by *not* comparing God's Empire with a cedar of Lebanon. Rather, he used the tiny seed of a shrub plant, a mustard seed, "the smallest of all the seeds," as a simile for God's Empire. Though technically there *are* smaller seeds, a mustard seed *is* very small and a mature bush never grows over a few feet high. It is like an aggressive weed that no one would plant near a garden, because it takes over and dominates as it spreads over the ground.

Yet it has positive, though unexpected, qualities. Although it is bitter, it was thought to have medicinal qualities for treating insect bites, fungi, and phlegm. And it was used for toothache and as a gargle. It cleared the senses and the bowels. Stephen Patterson says,

> Now that is a useful plant! The Empire of God may not be what you expected, but it is not without its qualities. It clears the head, penetrates the brain. It is good against all poisonous foes. It clears the throat, restores your voice. Calms your troubled soul. Clears the senses. Cleans you out (*God of Jesus*, 138).

God's Empire is not ruled by violence, constant fear, and war, as were the empires of Egypt and Rome. It is not like a great cedar of Lebanon. Rather, it is like a tiny mustard seed. It is not a tree at all, nor does it have sweet fruit. It is like weed that is very hard to control. That is what God's Empire is like.

In this strange way, Jesus spoke about God's Empire. But why would Jesus use such a simile?

We know what Jesus stood for, and it was not violence. Jesus did not try to build a great empire, nor exploit the hatred of enemies, nor promote the domination of other people. If one word can capture Jesus' message, it is *compassion*. When asked to sum up what God wants of us, Jesus answered *compassion*, or love (*agape*), for God and for other people. Compassion literally means "to feel or suffer *with*," to understand others, especially our enemies. It is so simple and seemingly small and common, just like a tiny mustard seed. And it is nothing like what we expect will make us feel safe and secure in an empire that lives by dominating other nations.

Comparing the Empire of God to a mustard seed would command the immediate attention of an audience of rural peasants because it is so unexpected. God was supposed to come as a conquering king to slay their enemies. Was this a joke? Well, yes, in a way – but a serious joke. To say that God's Empire is like a mustard seed was ridiculous and Robert Funk notes this parable's "comic effect" (*Five Gospels*, 484). But God's Empire is so unlike the hegemonic empires of Egypt and Rome that Jesus needed to use some shocking images to help people understand this. God's Empire of compassion, hope, and courage is the opposite of the violent empires ruled by hate, hopelessness, and fear, and which live by dominating other nations.

For the prophets of the Hebrew scriptures, like Ezekiel, and for Jesus, God is not found in violence and domination, but in compassion and mutual cooperation with others. It is in God's Empire, not in Egyptian, Roman, or even in American empires of fear, perpetual war, and violence, that we find God. God and God's Empire are not symbolized by a towering tree of pride and strutting arrogance, but by a tiny mustard seed of compassionate work for justice and peace.

1. *Name as many empires as you can.*
2. *How do/did they rule?*
3. *How is God's Empire different?*
4. *How would Jesus oppose the empires of our time?*
5. *What simile or metaphor would you use to describe God's Empire?*

~ 19 ~

The Absentee Landlord

WHAT DO YOU THINK?
Can oppressed people win their freedom using non-violence?

Mark 12:1–8

[1]Then he began to speak to them in parables. "A man planted a vineyard, put a fence around it, dug a pit for the wine press, and built a watch-tower; then he leased it to tenants and went to another country. [2]When the season came, he sent a slave to the tenants to collect from them his share of the produce of the vineyard. [3]But they seized him, and beat him, and sent him away empty-handed. [4]And again he sent another slave to them; this one they beat over the head and insulted. [5]Then he sent another, and that one they killed. And so it was with many others; some they beat, and others they killed. [6]He had still one other, a beloved son. Finally he sent him to them, saying, 'They will respect my son.' [7]But those tenants said to one another, 'This is the heir; come, let us kill him, and the inheritance will be ours.' [8]So they seized him, killed him, and threw him out of the vineyard. [9]What then will the owner of the vineyard do? He will come and destroy the tenants and give the vineyard to others.

Thomas 65

[1]A...person owned a vineyard and rented it to some farmers, as they could work it and he could collect its crop from them. [2]He sent his slave so the farmers would give him the vineyard's crop. [3]They grabbed him, beat him and almost killed him and the slave returned and told his master. [4]His master said, "Perhaps he didn't know them." [5]He sent another slave, and the farmers beat that one as well. [6]Then the master sent his son and said, "Perhaps they'll show my son some respect." [7]Because the farmers knew that he was the heir to the vineyard, they grabbed him and killed him. [8]Anyone here with two ears had better listen.

(See also Matthew 21:33–41, Luke 20: 9–18.)

A New Image

What images are possible for this parable? It is relatively long, with at least three scenes that illustrate three levels of violence: structural violence, rebellious violence, and reactionary violence. Because at least three images are needed, I chose a three-sided relief to illustrate the three levels of violence.

The first side represents the structural violence of a landlord establishing his vineyard as a cash crop, with sharecrop renters doing the work. He appears in the foreground, content with his ability to have the vineyard built, while he is absent. He would not have been a popular figure in a land where it was believed that God is the only true landowner, and where the peasant's allotments were being confiscated to "join house to house, and add land to land" (Isaiah 5:7–8) so that large estates could be formed for cash crops. This confiscation was, of course, legal if not just. Angry workers appear in the middle ground. In the distant background are the vineyard, fence, watch tower, and press.

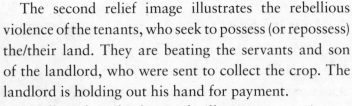

The second relief image illustrates the rebellious violence of the tenants, who seek to possess (or repossess) the/their land. They are beating the servants and son of the landlord, who were sent to collect the crop. The landlord is holding out his hand for payment.

Finally, the third panel illustrates reactionary violence, in which the Roman army is called in to crush the labourers. The landlord's thumbs-down gesture gives the go-ahead for the violence. A Roman commander holds his sword out to begin, and the soldiers march toward the vineyard for the kill.

Combined, the three panels illustrate the kinds of violence that typified the Roman empire. The "hidden" violence of the first panel, a structural level of violence, is rarely acknowledged. For example, the common name given this parable, the Wicked Tenants, already assumes that the tenants are the only "wicked" ones. So it helps to imagine such structural violence in clay and photography. The second level of rebellious violence happens out in the open, where all can see it. The third level of reactionary violence suggests the futility of the second level, violent rebellion, but also unmasks the cruelty of the first level, structural violence, which formed the foundation of Rome's empire.

Parable Research

This parable is usually called the "Wicked Tenants" because the tenants beat, humiliate, and even kill those sent to collect the harvest for the landowner. Obviously, they are condemned as wicked not only for refusing to pay their share of the shared crop, but also for violently resisting the collectors. The common view is that they must therefore pay the price for their violence and resistance.

Another common interpretation makes this parable an allegory, which all three synoptic writers used to interpret the parable to the early church. Allegory fits this parable like a glove. The landowner (God) sends his servants (prophets) and his son (Jesus), who are beaten and killed by the tenants (Jewish leaders). This allegory so interpreted has been used as a pretext for attacking Jews through Western history. Clearly, none of us now would use the parable for such anti-Semitism, but as an allegory it becomes all too easy to do so. Because all three synoptic gospel writers interpreted Jesus' parable in this way, I have gone to Thomas' version of the parable, which does not use such allegory.

Thomas gives the story straight. He ends the parable with the killing of the son and simply says by way of interpretation, "Anyone with two ears had better listen." Some scholars, though not all, see Thomas' version to be closer to the version Jesus might have told, since Jesus often left parables open-ended without an overlay of interpretation.

Thomas' non-allegorical version encourages us to explore more of the social, economic, and political background of first-century Palestine. In this way, we may come closer to what Jesus might have been saying in the parable.

Consideration of this background often begins with the obvious fact that Jesus was crucified by the Romans because he was a threat to their rule. If he had preached only about otherworldly matters, they would have left him alone, as they did many other preachers at that time. To threaten Rome enough to the point where they would crucify him, Jesus must have gone way beyond proclaiming strictly private spirituality. In fact, Luke 4:18 tell us that he preached "good news to the poor," "release to the captives," and freedom for the oppressed ("let the oppressed go free").

Assuming, then, that Jesus threatened the economic, social, and political order, how exactly does this apply to the parable of the absentee landlord and the tenants? Under Roman rule, the economy was being rapidly commercialized. Palestinian farmers were losing their land – land they considered to be a divine gift to them, a sacred trust forever. They survived on what would be called "subsistence farming" today, as opposed to commercial farming. But urban elites, through taxation and debt servitude, often foreclosed on the farmers leaving them to become sharecroppers at best, or day labourers, beggars, tax collectors, or prostitutes at worst. After confiscating peasant land, the elites would build large estates and grow cash crops, such as wine grapes to export, using for labour the same sharecropper tenants who had been forced off their land. Given this context, we can see what motivated the tenants to rebel.

William Herzog once named the landlord (not the tenants) as the wicked one in this parable (*Subversive Speech*, 98–113).[1] In doing so, he used the concept of the three levels of violence, from Dom Helder Camara's book *Spiral of Violence*, to untangle this parable. Level one is structural violence, such as the expropriation of the farmer's land, which was legal. Remember, however, that it was the *expropriators* who wrote the laws that made it legal. Level two is the rebellious violence of the tenants, which is a response to the oppression and systemic violence of level one. Level three is the violent reaction of the elite establishment, which crushes this rebellion. Reactionary violence is legal violence, but it is not *justice*. As Herzog says,

> They were peasants pushed over the edge of survival, and they were heirs of Yahweh's allotment of land whose inheritance had been stolen from them. Their violent outburst was their way of reasserting their honourable status as heirs, not the shameful act of usurpers. Yet the ruling elites portrayed themselves as Yahweh's rightful heirs and the rebellious peasants as outlaws (*Subversive Speech*, 112).

The landowners were doing what Isaiah preached against, when he said God "expected justice, but saw bloodshed; righteousness, but heard a cry! Ah, you who join house to house, who add field to field, until there is room for no one but you..." (5:7–8). Joining fields was done by expropriating the land, which was made legal by self-serving laws that protected only the elites.

Understanding Camara's three levels of violence and how they interrelate[2] does not justify the violence of the tenants (level two), but it does show how violent the first level of structural/legal violence, which is usually ignored, really is. It also shows the futility of level-two violence.

How can all three levels of violence be avoided? Maybe that is what Jesus was getting at in this parable, which seems to illustrate how violence is futile and how it always ends badly. There is a better way, which Jesus preached throughout the gospels.[3] Perhaps the parable pushes us to look harder for such non-violent tools for ending conflict.

Questions for Discussion

1. *Which do you prefer and why: the allegorical interpretation, or the interpretation that takes into account an understanding of the levels of violence?*

2. *This parable has been used to justify anti-Semitism. How might acts of anti-Semitic violence against Jews in Europe and North America today fit into the levels of violence defined by Dom Helder Camara?*

3. *How might Camara's and Richard Horsley's (see footnote 2) understanding of the levels of violence help us to make sense of the violence between Palestinians and Jews in the Middle East today?*

4. *Can you think of examples of comparable expropriations and debt slavery today? Where and how do these take place?*

---

[1] However, Herzog changed his mind in his more recent book, *Prophet and Teacher*. He sees the Landowner as God, the tenants as the local elites and the servants as the prophets and Jesus whom the local elites killed. I prefer his earlier non-allegorical interpretation.

[2] Richard Horsley, in his early book called *Jesus and the Spiral of Violence: Popular Jewish Resistance in Roman Palestine,* adds two more levels of violence to Camara's three. Between level one (structural violence) and level two (violent rebellion) he adds non-violent resistance and reactionary repression. In the many uprisings he studied, it was only after the peasant's non-violent resistance failed that violent resistance was then applied. However, in a significant number of cases, non-violent resistance by Jews against Roman occupation actually succeeded.

[3] Note especially Matthew 18:15–17, which lists concrete steps in non-violent conflict resolution.

Parables in
The Gospel of Matthew

~ 20 ~

The Two Builders

WHAT DO YOU THINK?
Is it enough for a Christian to hear and proclaim that Jesus is Lord?

Matthew 7:21–27

[21]Not everyone who says to me, "Lord, Lord," will enter the kingdom of heaven, but only the one who does the will of my Father in heaven. [22]On that day many will say to me, "Lord, Lord, did we not prophesy in your name, and cast out demons in your name, and do many deeds of power in your name?" [23]Then I will declare to them, "I never knew you; go away from me, you evildoers." [24]Everyone then who hears these words of mine and acts on them will be like a wise man who built his house on rock. [25]The rain fell, the floods came, and the winds blew and beat on that house, but it did not fall, because it had been founded on rock. [26]And everyone who hears these words of mine and does not act on them will be like a foolish man who built his house on sand. [27]The rain fell, and the floods came, and the winds blew and beat against that house, and it fell – and great was its fall!

(See also Luke 6:47–49.)

A New Image

The house built on a firm rock foundation rather than on sand is a well-known image, but the challenge of communicating this parable without words is great. The house with a rock foundation is simple enough. In my sculpture, the strong pillars underneath the house show that it stands amidst the rushing flood, which appears in the bottom foreground. Streams of blowing rain and smoke blowing horizontally from the chimney suggest the violence of the storm.

But how do we depict that this parable is about human behaviour and that the weather and buildings are metaphors for that behaviour? Note that the man's legs are shaped like pillars, echoing the strong pillars under the standing house. The doing of Jesus' word is symbolized by the way the man shelters the child in his arms. For Matthew, hearing and speaking the words of Jesus were not enough. We must *do* good deeds, such as sheltering the young.

Working the imagery backwards, the good deed of caring for the young is symbolized by the strong foundation of the house, which resists the turbulent storm. This is side one of the two-sided relief.

On side two, a bewildered man wonders what is happening to him, as he is blown about by the storm. His robe and hair blow in the wind. He does not seem to realize the cause of his misery, which was his foolish decision to build on a weak, sand foundation. The flood has washed away his house, a dog seeks a dry spot on a roof, and even the chimney is blowing away in the driving rain and wind. Only good deeds provide a solid foundation. Without good deeds, talk is useless.

Parable Research

This parable appears in both Matthew and Luke and is thus considered to be from the Q source, which is common to both of them. Matthew locates the parable right after the Sermon on the Mountain; Luke places it right after the Sermon on the Plain. Both seem to suggest by this location that these sermons of Jesus are the firm foundation on which to build our lives. If we don't act on these sermons, we are like the bewildered man whose house crumbles in the flood. The message seems clear enough, yet there are some issues to resolve.

First, is the parable from Jesus? A number of scholars doubt its authenticity and therefore ignore it. But John Donahue is more positive: "Clearly...there is a widely based tradition, going back to Jesus, which describes authentic religion as 'hearing and doing'" (137). Indeed, the Hebrew Bible often stresses that to really hear God's word we must *do* it. Note, for example, "All that the Lord has spoken we will do" (Exodus 24:7). Joachim Jeremias says that the comparison of the rock and the sand suggests that the parable is authentically from Jesus, because he frequently used such pairings (70–71). Barbara Reid elaborates on the other contrasting pairings in the parable itself: for example, saying or doing, and hearing or doing. Also, the gospel "contrasts saying 'Lord, Lord' with doing God's will" (*Matthew*, *Year A*, 64). Clearly, the necessity of *doing* and not just *hearing* or *repeating* Jesus' words is part of the authentic Jesus tradition.

In other words, if Jesus were here today, he would probably tell us that we have to "walk the talk," or "walk the walk." According to this parable, only the "walk" or the deeds give clear evidence that one has truly heard the words of Jesus, has committed to live them in one's life, and has actually risked the time or money or energy to make one's life fit the justice, peace, and blessedness of God's Empire.

Let's look back at the Sermon on the Mountain, which spells out what God's Empire is about and what exactly we are called to hear and do. It begins in chapter 5 with the Beatitudes, which do not say "God Bless

America," or "Canada," or any other nation state. Rather, they say God bless the poor, the mourners, the meek, the hungry, the pure in heart, the peacemakers, the persecuted, and the falsely accused. Matthew's Jesus tells us to be a light to the world. He calls us to join him in fulfilling the Torah and the prophets. He warns against anger and conflict, which should be settled even before one makes an offering to God. Jesus rejects the ease with which a man can commit adultery and get a divorce. He opposes swearing and all distortions of speech. He calls us to love our enemies rather than take revenge, and to practise piety, prayer, fasting, and charity, without making a big show of it. He warns that money won't lead to happiness or blessedness, or that worrying won't help anything. He tells us that it is not our job to judge others' sins, but only to remove the sin in ourselves. Rather than judge, we are to treat others the way we want to be treated, and to honour God. Finally, he sums up everything using two parables: one about a good tree that bears good fruit and the other about a house built on a stone foundation.

Clearly, the meaning of the latter parable is that we have to do, or avoid doing, all the things Jesus said in the Sermon on the Mountain. Doing does not mean simply hearing Jesus' words or even *preaching* them. Most important, doing does not mean saying flattering words about Jesus (saying "Lord, Lord") or even *worshipping* Jesus. Even if you yell "Lord, Lord," and prophesy, and exorcize demons, and make a big deal of your deeds of power – even if you do all these things but still do not *do* what Jesus asks, then you will be left out of God's Empire.

"Hear, heed, and do" is the sound bite for this parable. Its simple words are balanced by the extreme difficulty of actually *acting* on the message contained in the Sermon on the Mountain. Archibald Hunter sums up the plain meaning of the parable: obey me and you will weather the storm; neglect these words and you court disaster (74).

The contrasting verbal images of a house built on rock and a house built on sand make our calling to do God's Empire hard to mistake, yet we do so daily. By visualizing these two buildings and by sculpting them in clay, I hope that I have at least guided myself to build a stronger foundation from which to live my life.

1. *Which items in the Sermon on the Mountain do you find easiest to do? Which items to you find hardest to do?*
2. *How is God's Empire different from Rome's empire? How is it different from our own government?*
3. *In what ways do we say, "Lord, Lord," and then not do what Jesus calls us to do?*
4. *Give examples of "walking the talk" (or "walking the walk," which means the same thing).*

~ 21 ~

The Wheat and the Tares

WHAT DO YOU THINK?
Do we hurt ourselves when we judge and exclude others as evil?

Matthew 13:24–30

[24]He put before them another parable: "The kingdom of heaven may be compared to someone who sowed good seed in his field; [25]but while everybody was asleep, an enemy came and sowed weeds among the wheat, and then went away. [26]So when the plants came up and bore grain, then the weeds appeared as well. [27]And the slaves of the householder came and said to him, 'Master, did you not sow good seed in your field? Where, then, did these weeds come from?' [28]He answered, 'An enemy has done this.' The slaves said to him, 'Then do you want us to go and gather them?' [29]But he replied, 'No; for in gathering the weeds you would uproot the wheat along with them. [30]Let both of them grow together until the harvest; and at harvest time I will tell the reapers, Collect the weeds first and bind them in bundles to be burned, but gather the wheat into my barn.'"

A New Vision

How can we imagine this parable? A servant is ready to attack the weeds; but the owner prevents the attack.

He allows the wheat and tares (good and evil) to grow together, and leaves the judgement, separation, and exclusion to other beings and to another time.

In my sculpture, the householder and the slave are presented in a simple relief image that allows the extended hoe and hands and arms to "speak."

Matthew seems to have Jesus say, "When we presume to know who is evil and to cut them out, we (who are presumed to be good, because we judge ourselves to be good) will damage ourselves in the process" – just as the householder warns the worker that his weeding will kill the good wheat plants along with the weeds. In other words, we cannot finally know good and evil. Even Adam and Eve were told they are not "like God, knowing good and evil." But they tried to be like God anyway, and were thus sent out of the Garden of Eden (Genesis 3:5, 22). The sculptural image suggests the wisdom of not trying to play God, who alone judges good and evil.

Parable Research

Matthew calls this parable "the weeds of the field" (Matthew 23:36), but it is also know as The Wheat and the Tares. Tares are toxic weeds also known as darnel. They look similar to wheat and are, therefore, hard to separate. Some scholars agree with the servant that an early weeding of tares is wise, because the roots go deeper and entangle with those of the wheat as they grow. Once tares are mixed with the wheat grain at harvest, the crop is spoiled. However, these are literal, agricultural details, whereas the parable is a metaphor for the mixture of good and evil in the human community. For Matthew, that community would be the early church. The central issue, then, is *who* will separate out the evil people from the good people in our communities, and *when* will they do this.

This parable is unique to Matthew, although there is a short version of it in the non-canonical Gospel of Thomas (57). Most scholars, however, observe that Thomas relies on Matthew's version. They also note that Matthew appears to replace the Seed and Harvest parable in Mark with this one, for Matthew takes over Mark's text on both sides of this Wheat and Tares parable, but leaves out the Seed and Harvest parable itself.

The Wheat and Tares parable is followed by two other parables: the Mustard Seed and the Leaven. After these, Matthew adds an allegorical interpretation of the Wheat and Tares, in which Jesus explains its meaning to the disciples (Matthew 13:36–43), but not to the crowds, whom he leaves without an explanation (Matthew 13:34).

In this allegory, the field is the world, the good seeds are children of the kingdom, the weeds or tares are the children of the evil one, and the enemy is the devil. The harvest represents the end of the age, when angels will separate the evil from the good, and cast the evil into the furnace where there is crying and gnashing of teeth. Most scholars believe that Matthew added this allegorical interpretation and that it does not come from Jesus. C. H. Dodd dismissed it thus: "We shall do well to forget this interpretation as completely as possible" (148).

Joachim Jeremias agrees, saying that Matthew's allegory "passes over in silence the obvious motive of the parable, namely, the exhortation to patience" (64). Jeremias records 36 examples of Matthew's hand in the allegory. Then he concludes that the original purpose (the call to patience) "has been turned in Matthew [into]...a description of the Last Judgment" (67).

Scholarly consensus since Dodd and Jeremias follows their lead and goes directly to the parable itself without the allegorical interpretation. There, the issue is who will separate good and evil, and when. Granted, even to interpret the weeds as evil people and the wheat as good people is the beginning of allegory, but this is a much more limited, metaphorical translation.

What are we to make of the question of who weeds out evil? The servants initially approach the householder to report the presence of the weeds and there is a short exchange about who might have planted them, an act the owner blames on an unknown enemy. Then the servants offer to gather the weeds in. The owner says "no" to the servant's offer, for it would damage the wheat to pull out the weeds.

A common interpretation is that good and evil are mixed together in life, and it is not our job to separate out the evil. We live with it not only in others, but in ourselves. Another way to put this is that we are not to judge good and evil, but to leave that to God. Such an interpretation would be consistent with Paul's writings, where he says we are "not to judge others" (Romans 2:1 and 14:13). The only beings allowed to separate good from evil are the angels, and they do not do this now but at the end of the age. The harvest is a common symbol throughout the Bible for the end of time and for judgement day. This answers the second question of *when* the separation is to happen. It happens at the harvest or the end of time.

Matthews adds his punishment to this scenario: the "furnace of fire, where there will be weeping and gnashing of their teeth." However, if we focus on the parable itself rather than on Matthew's allegorical interpretation, we can appreciate the value of not attempting to separate and exclude people whom we might consider evil. First of all, we are not wise enough to make such judgements about the degree of evil and good in another person, nor even about the degree of evil and good in ourselves. We are all a mixture of good and evil. As Paul says, "There is no one who is righteous" (Romans 3:10).

Second, Jesus' historical context included the Essenes and the Pharisees, two religious groups that were very exclusive. By contrast, Jesus refused to exclude and separate people. Rather, Jesus' overall message was one of inclusion and of extravagant welcome.

We have gradually learned how interpersonal relations improve when we avoid judgement. For example, this wisdom from the first century has surfaced in our time in psychological therapy, which avoids judgement and thereby helps a person move beyond condemnation and exclusion. Even so, we don't always follow our own best wisdom. Those who make war know very well that violence becomes easier and more acceptable when we label our enemies as evil, and so they encourage their soldiers to engage in this kind of labelling. At home, demonizing one's opponents has become a common tool in political campaigns.

But if we are to love our enemies as Jesus taught, we cannot consider them evil weeds to cut down.

Questions for Discussion

1. *What do you make of the dismissal by scholars of Matthew's allegorical interpretation?*
2. *Is the separation of good and evil by people possible or impossible in this life?*
3. *What happens when we condemn others as evil?*

~ 22 ~

The Leaven

WHAT DO YOU THINK?
Can God's Empire of abundance for all come to us in unholy ways?

Matthew 13:33

He told them another parable: "the kingdom of heaven is like yeast that a woman took and mixed in with three measures of flour until all of it was leavened."

(See also Luke 13:20–21.)

Thomas 96

Jesus said, "The kingdom of the father is like [a certain] woman. She took a little leaven, [concealed] it in some dough, and made it into large loaves. Let him who has ears hear."

A New Image

I imagine a woman on one side of a relief sculpture putting a lump of leaven in three large, basket-sized containers. She leans over to mix the leaven into the grain baskets, her posture stylized.

She has a mischievous look and smile, suggesting that she is doing something unconventional.

On the second side of the relief, she is filled with joy at the results – an explosion of bread ready to feed her whole village so that all have enough to eat. God's Empire is the place of love where all have enough.

Granted, the text makes no mention of a huge pile of bread, but it is the obvious result of "three measures" plus leaven, which Jesus' listeners would have known is a huge amount. I have spelled this out and pictured it for us moderns, who may not know the background or the oral tradition that was available to Jesus' audience.

Parable Research

This short parable is often called "The Leaven in the Loaf," but it should be plural *loaves*. That's because three measures of grain – about 50 lbs or 22.5 kg – plus leaven or yeast, would rise to an enormous mound of dough, and produce many loaves of bread when baked.

This comparison of the Empire of God to leavened bread is one of a few very odd similes Jesus made. The other strange similes are found in the Lost Coin, Lost Sheep, Prodigal Son, Pearl Merchant, and Mustard Seed parables. The very strangeness of the comparisons is a criterion some scholars use to confirm that these parables originated with Jesus and were not created by the gospel writers.

Both Matthew and Luke report nearly identical versions, except Matthew typically uses the phrase "kingdom of heaven" while Luke uses "kingdom of God." Thomas has a similar version, though "father" replaces "heaven" and "God"; and the realm of the father is compared directly with a woman rather than with the leaven itself. Also, Thomas draws attention to the small quantity of leaven and to the largeness of the loaves, just as he draws attention to the "largest" sheep in his version of the Lost Sheep parable.

Matthew locates this parable in what is called the "parable discourses," which are seven parables strung together. It is considered a "twin" to the Mustard Seed parable. Luke locates the parable in his "travel narrative." The parable is not found in Mark and, therefore, is usually thought to be from the Q source, which both Matthew and Luke used.

The most notable aspect of this parable is the radical comparison of God's Empire with an unclean fungus, leaven. (Our modern-day yeast, which comes in a package, is a leaven.) Judaism viewed unleavened bread as clean, and leavened bread as unclean. Unleavened bread is still the bread of choice for the ritual that commemorates the exodus of the Hebrews from Egypt. According to the biblical account, because of the hurriedness of their flight, they could not wait for the leavened dough to rise, so they baked flat, unleavened bread for their journey out of slavery.

Leaven causes fermentation, which leads to the gaseous expansion of the dough and, when baked, to the risen bread. Leaven came to be considered a corruption of the bread, but also a symbol for moral corruption, as when Jesus warns against the "yeast of the Pharisees and Sadducees" (Matthew 16:6). Also, Paul speaks of cleaning out the "yeast of malice and evil" and of replacing it with "the unleavened bread of sincerity and truth" (1 Corinthians 5:7–8). Why would Jesus compare God's Empire with corruption?

Jesus used the same strange technique in the Lost Coin parable, when he compared a woman to God, or to God's Empire. Given the patriarchal society in which Jesus lived, many within his audience would have found this parable highly offensive. Why would he make such a comparison?

As usual, scholars disagree on the meaning of this parable, and the gospel writers did not interpret it as they often did other parables. But as with its "twin" parable, the Mustard Seed, Jesus seems to make a shocking comparison to move his audience beyond their conventional expectations, which were that God is like a mighty warrior king, or like a giant cedar tree. "No," Jesus seems to say. "God's Empire is like a tiny mustard seed." In this parable, God's Empire is once again found where it is least expected – mixed in like corruption, by a woman who makes a pile of leavened bread.

Here is one way to interpret this parable. Think of God's Empire not as modelled after a dominating, wilful king or an emperor who rules by violence. Rather, think of God's Empire after the model of Jesus who lived by love. Now the parable's strangeness begins to make sense. Women in Jesus' time were virtually powerless in earthly terms and rarely ruled anything beyond the household, if that. If they had any control at all, they had to wield it without violence. An empire governed by non-violent love would have contrasted sharply with the dominating Roman conquerors, and with the priestly purity codes, which declared that much of what the poor could do was unclean. But love builds no such boundaries. Like the leaven, it works invisibly to raise the bread of life to its fullness. Love includes all and insists that there be bread for all. Love provides what all people need to live.

1. What is your vision of God's Empire or kingdom?
2. Why would Jesus compare God's Empire to small things like yeast and seeds?
3. Thomas' Jesus compares God's Empire to a woman putting leaven in dough. Is that different or the same as Luke and Matthew's comparison with the yeast itself? Explain.
4. Is it reasonable to suggest that a great abundance of food to feed her village would come from the woman's action even though it is not in the text? If not, what other meaning does it have?

~ 23 ~

The Treasure and The Pearl Merchant

WHAT DO YOU THINK?
Can we earn the joy of God's Empire by sacrificing and working for it?

Matthew 13:44–46

[44]The kingdom of heaven is like treasure hidden in a field, which someone found and hid; then in his joy he goes and sells all that he has and buys that field. [45]Again, the kingdom of heaven is like a merchant in search of fine pearls; [46]on finding one pearl of great value, he went and sold all that he had and bought it.

(See also Thomas 109 and 76.)

A New Image

These twin parables suggest two, two-sided relief sculptures. On the first side of the first sculpture, the treasure finder discovers a treasure in a field. The treasure is shaped like a large vase and is buried underground – a common way valuables were hidden in Jesus' time.

The vase shape is represented by negative space, which suggests that something eternal, holy, or demonic might reside there. The empty space also extends beyond the confines of the earthly clay, which once again hints at something "other than" our usual experience. The person has found it and seeks to cover it. Then he will buy the field. He has an appearance of doing something unethical, if not illegal.

On the second side of the first sculpture, he has sold all that he has in order to buy the field and to get the treasure. The fact that he has truly sold *everything* is symbolized by his clothing, or rather, his lack of it.

He is filled with joy and dances over his found treasure, a holy gift of blessing.

On the second relief, the pearl merchant also comes upon the most valuable gift of God's Empire, symbolized as a pearl of great price. On side one, he is well-dressed, with a fur coat and hat, and with rings on his fingers. He has a business-as-usual look as he fiddles with his wealth of jewels.

But on the second side of the relief, he too has sold all that he has, even his clothing, to buy this precious pearl, the Empire of God. The pearl is adored so much that it figuratively becomes his eye, or the joyous perspective by which he now sees the rest of the world. The exchange has been worth it, because he now has the wealth he had previously striven for unsuccessfully – that is, a sense of self-worth sought through the accumulation of wealth.

This is a treasure worth everything, yet he (and we) cannot earn it. It comes by grace or faith alone. It becomes the new vision for his (and our) life.

Parable Research

These two short parables are usually considered twins. (Sometimes the Fishnet parable, which follows immediately after, is also considered alongside them.) They appear only in Matthew, but Thomas has two similar parables, to which he has added interpretations. In Thomas' versions, the person who finds the *treasure* digs it up and becomes a moneylender. Thomas makes the person who finds the *pearl* an example of seeking first the treasures of heaven, where moth or worms cannot destroy.

Matthew provides no immediate application or interpretation, but puts these parables in the larger context of Jesus' explanation the Weeds in the Field parable (Matthew 13:24–30). Matthew frames the parables – including now the Fishnet parable – with his typical separation of the good from the evil at the end of the age, when the evil will suffer "the furnace of fire, where there will be weeping and gnashing of teeth" (v. 49–50).

Most scholars attempt to go behind Matthew's framing in order to discover what Jesus may have meant, though, as John Donahue says, they "admit of multiple interpretations" (68). For example, a common interpretation is that the disciples, like the treasure finder and the pearl merchant, are to sacrifice "all" or everything for the Empire of God. C. H. Dodd sums up the logic in this way:

> You agree that the Kingdom of God is the highest good: it is within your power to possess it here and now, if, like the treasure-finder and the pearl-merchant, you will throw caution to the winds: "Follow me!" (87).

However, this interpretation, which calls for the sacrificing of "caution" and "all," has some doubters, whose thoughts we will explore after a further word on the context of these two parables.

Since there were no banks or ATMs in Jesus' time, it was not unusual for people to bury their valuables in the ground. In fact, the parable of the talents is another example of this practice. The possibility that one might discover such a treasure would have been something the disciples were familiar with. The wealthy pearl merchant, on the other hand, would have been less within their experience – though they would likely have had knowledge of such people and would have viewed their wealth negatively, considering they were only poor peasants themselves. At the time, pearls were like gold, if not even more precious. John of Patmos imagined them as the construction material for heaven's "pearly gates" (Revelation 21:21).

Scholars often discuss the ethical issue surrounding the devious act of the treasure finder, who covers the treasure and then buys the field, presumably so that he can have it to himself rather than share it with the field's owner. John Dominic Crossan sums up the logic of this ethically dubious behaviour in his book *Finding Is the First Act*, which is entirely dedicated to this parable. He says, "If the treasure belongs to the finder, buying the land is unnecessary. But, if the treasure does not belong to the finder, buying the land is unjust" (91). So the fact that treasure finder bought the field implicates him in an ethically dubious act. Yet this does not destroy the value of the parable, for Jesus said many things and told other parables in which the subject and/or the behaviour were considered corrupt, for example, the Leaven and the Unjust Steward parables.

Bernard Brandon Scott expands this discussion to include the pearl merchant, who buys the pearl of great value. Scott says that because the pearl has no ultimate value, the merchant must sell it in order to live, as he would have been broke, having sold everything to acquire it in the first place.

> The kingdom cannot be possessed as a value in itself, "alone for himself," …for the merchant will sooner or later have to sell his pearl. And that is the kingdom's corrupting power – the desire to possess it (319).

For Scott, the fact that the pearl merchant sells everything in order to acquire the pearl is "a sign of God's grace working outside the laws of the everyday" (402). In other words, both parables suggest that God's grace operates beyond the law, and both suggest that the kingdom can bring not only immeasurable joy, but also possible corruption.

Other scholars dismiss the ethical issue contained in the Treasure parable as it would "hardly have been germane to the telling of the parable" (Hultgren, 415). This view seems convincing, because parables are not moral lessons, but rather short stories about God's Empire (about what it is and what it is not). They use rogues (the corrupt judge) and fools (the rich farmer) to make their point.

It is helpful to note that there are both similarities and dissimilarities between these two parables. To name their similarities, both use similes to compare everyday situations and actions to God's Empire. Both call for total commitment – the selling of all to attain the kingdom of heaven. Both use questionable acts to make the point. That is, lusting after treasures (or jewellery) on earth is tantamount to "laying up treasures on earth," which Jesus elsewhere rejects in favour of laying up treasures in heaven (Matthew 6:19–20).

To name the differences between the parables, the similes for God's Empire do not correspond with each other – in the first parable, the kingdom is compared to the treasure, but in the second parable it is compared to the merchant. Also, in the first parable the treasure is found by chance, but in the second parable the pearl is perhaps found as the result of a deliberate search (*how* the merchant found the pearl is not stated). Moving on, the *treasure* is found by "someone," most likely not a rich person, whereas the *pearl* is found by a wealthy merchant. Only the treasure finder displays "joy," though the merchant may have experienced it as well. Finally, the treasure finder hides his prize, whereas the merchant does not.

Now we return to the most common interpretation of these parables, which sees them as a call for sacrifice. Rudolf Bultmann says of selling *all* for the treasure and the pearl,

> "For the sake of the Kingdom of God" involves complete renunciation, brings every man face to face with the ultimate *Either*-Or. To decide for the Kingdom is to sacrifice for it all things else (*Jesus*, 31).

Bultmann gave this interpretation of these two parables in 1934. Ernst Fuchs, a student of Bultmann, later rejected this interpretation by saying, "There is no mention of a sacrifice" in the parables. Rather,

> we should place our whole trust in the one word which proclaims God's coming... The Basileia comes to those who believe in it and who allow for their faith no other object – just as the men in the [parables] wanted nothing other than their treasure and their pearls.

Thus, only faith – "all one can muster" – not sacrifice, is required (Fuchs, 94–95). Fuchs concludes that these parables call us to *do nothing*,

> because God has already acted...finding [as in finding a treasure] is itself primarily "non action" – not a work or a deed, but an event that happens to me... Did Paul not reject justification by works simply because it had become superfluous...? (Fuchs, 130).

To be fair, Bultmann says both: The Reign of God "is a miracle independent of every human act," but he also says it "requires sacrifice" (*Theology, volume I*, 8–9).

In Fuchs' interpretation, selling everything is a sacrifice because it amounts to a work, a deed done to earn God's favour. Rather, we are called by Jesus in these parables to renounce our striving after treasures and our collecting of things on earth – to stop *doing* and seeking to have things. Instead, we are called to focus on *being*: being at rest, doing nothing to earn God's Empire. In the parables, the gift of the kingdom came to both men despite the fact that they weren't doing anything extraordinary, but were simply going about their daily lives.

Another example of finding God's Empire without earning it or sacrificing for it might be a person who is haunted by a lack of self-worth, one who lives in shame. He or she tries to cover or medicate the pain of this shame by collecting honours, wealth, friends, achievements, and a wholesome family. The person becomes famous, admired, rich in all the ways available to us (see Tolstoy's *The Death of Ivan Illich*). Yet the person keeps striving for more, as if after a drug, in order to cover his or her underlying sense of unworthiness and shame. Finally, one day, the person falls ill and can do nothing but remain passive and receive help. In this new state, the person can only *receive* the word of God's Empire, of being already accepted, worthy, and without shame; of no longer needing to strive for worth. Like the treasure finder and the pearl merchant, this person is given already the greatest treasure possible – his or her worthiness, and the blessing of rest from striving to gain that worth.

This gift is worth everything and it is already given; it is not attainable by more striving and sacrifice. In the parables, the *finding* of the treasure and the pearl *precedes* the decision and effort to sell "all." But the treasure of worthiness (of living without shame, and of being accepted for who one already is) is *worth* selling everything for, even though it is already found. As already mentioned, John Dominic Crossan names his book on the Treasure parable *Finding Is the First Act*. Indeed, we have to *stop doing* and *start being*. Then we will do great things for the right reasons.

Questions for Discussion

1. *What do you think of the traditional view that we must sacrifice all or everything for God?*
2. *Do you think the treasure finder acts unethically when he hides the treasure?*
3. *Do you think making a faith-related personal sacrifice is always something we do to earn God's favour, or might there be other reasons for making such a sacrifice?*
4. *What do you think of the idea that we can reach God's Empire by doing nothing?*
5. *Does having faith mean doing nothing?*

~ 24 ~

The Fishnet

WHAT DO YOU THINK?
Is it right or possible for people to judge others as good or evil?

Matthew 13:47–50

[47]Again, the kingdom of heaven is like a net that was thrown into the sea and caught fish of every kind; [48]when it was full, they drew it ashore, sat down, and put the good into baskets but threw out the bad. [49]So it will be at the end of the age. The angels will come out and separate the evil from the righteous [50]and throw them into the furnace of fire, where there will be weeping and gnashing of teeth.

Thomas 8:1–4

The human one is like a wise fisherman who cast his net into the sea and drew it up from the sea full of little fish. Among them the wise fisherman discovered a fine large fish. He threw all the little fish back into the sea, and easily chose the large fish. Anyone here with two good ears had better listen!

A New Image

How can we picture this parable? If we follow most scholars and drop Matthew's addition of the "furnace of fire," then we may focus on transferring the job of sorting good people from evil people (i.e., condemning or blessing) to other-worldly beings (angels). If we humans are relieved of that job, then a basic justification for violence is removed. To portray this, I have created a two-sided relief sculpture. On the first side, we see a boat in the distance. A fishnet, in which all kinds of fish have been gathered, is being pulled into the boat.

The fish are a great mixture of edible and inedible, normal and odd-looking creatures, suggesting that we humans are also a collection of all kinds, good and bad, all mixed up together.

On the second side of the relief, angels (with small wings that merely hint that they are not human beings) are busily working away at hauling in and sorting the fish. One is lifting the net, while another is tossing some (perhaps the bad) out of the sculpture plane, symbolizing the separation of evil. The "good" are held up to honour. Like the fish on side one, these are stylized figures that discourage literalism. The sun on side one becomes a pulley on side two.

The message is clear: "Leave the sorting to the angels."

Parable Research

Once again, the Empire of God is compared to an everyday object or event – this time to a fishnet cast into the sea. This parable is unique to Matthew, though he includes other parables that are similar to this one. It follows immediately The Treasure and The Pearl Merchant. All three parables are addressed to the disciples rather than to the crowds.

There is a shorter fishnet parable in Thomas, but it is very different. It lacks Matthew's typical judgement, where the evil and the good are separated by the angels. Also, in Thomas' parable the comparison is not between the kingdom of heaven or the Empire of God and the fishnet, but, rather, between "the human one" and "a wise fisherman" who keeps only the "fine, large fish." In Thomas, the rest are thrown "back into the sea," instead of being "thrown away" as in Matthew.

Scholars such as Robert Funk, Bernard Brandon Scott, and James R. Butts (*Parables of Jesus*, note 70) believe that Thomas' parable may be based on Aesop. Others note Thomas' Gnostic wisdom in the phrase "wise fisherman." Still other scholars doubt that either version goes back to Jesus. Matthew's parable, they say, is about setting social boundaries in the early Christian community. In many ways, it parallels the parable of the Wheat and the Tares – that is, the good and evil are sorted out by the angels at the close of the age.

Whether or not this parable originates with Jesus, we can still appreciate the theme of angels rather than humans separating good and evil. Until the age to come, good and evil will remain mixed together.

The subtext here is that good and evil exist not only in the secular world, but also in our religious communities and within ourselves as well. The image of a fishnet, which Arland Hultgren translates as "dragnet," suggests a wide, all-inclusive net sweeping the sea from a boat, rather than a small, shoreline fishing net (305). The large net brings in all kinds of fish just as the church brings in all kinds of people. None is excluded in the net or at the church door. We live with the good and the bad all blended together. Good and bad co-exist like different fish in the sea. Good fish in the Bible were ones that were edible and clean, as determined by the law in Leviticus 11:9–12 and Deuteronomy 14:9. Unclean fish were judged to be those without fins or scales, such as eels.

As I noted in the Wheat and Tares parable, the bad tares are not weeded out from the good wheat either by the servants or by the landowner. The observation that only the angels should do the sorting easily remains an obscure, other-worldly generalization until we unpack the subtext. Let's look at how we ignore this injunction and why we should not.

How often do we dismiss certain people as hopelessly corrupt, beyond redemption, or simply bad, on the one hand; and, on the other hand, assume that other people are good and without fault of any kind, worthy of privileges, honour, and celebrity, if not worship. In making the first judgement, we "demonize" others; in making the second judgement, we "romanticize" or "sentimentalize" them. Both attitudes are very easy and convenient to assume. By demonizing some as evil enemies, they become "fair game." We can end the relationship, attack, and even harm or kill them. By romanticizing or sentimentalizing others, we grant them undue credit and even hold them up as flawless, saintly, or wise beyond criticism. We idolize them. Of course, we ourselves are usually first among the flawless, good people.

Most of us who think of ourselves as civilized and morally upright people would never kill or torture other people. Yet, in the United States, we allow our government to do so, and we pay dearly in taxes for such "defence." We pay executioners and other agents to torture and kill others, whom we (or our honourable leaders) have demonized as enemies, as evil.

The taking of another human life in self-defence is accepted in our courts as just. Such righteous self-defence is taken to the international level when our leaders declare a national emergency requiring an army to provide for our national self-defence. We readily comply – even to the point of risking our own lives – and usually feel quite patriotic in doing so. For the sake of our own "defence," we even risk the lives of our youth and willingly send them, if need be, to kill other people whom our leaders declare to be evil enemies. Within this logic, killing other people is judged acceptable, even righteous and heroic. We act like God, sorting the good (us) from the evil (them), and declare that the evil "them" deserve to be "thrown into the furnace of fire." Of course, national leaders also have another motive for war-making. Going to war is one way for them to keep and increase their power. This logic is so common and so routine that we often overlook it.

This parable of the everyday fishermen sorting good and bad fish in Matthew, or small and large fish in Thomas, comes with a powerful message. That message is exactly consistent with Jesus' teaching to "love our enemies" (Luke 6:27), not to sort them out and kill them. Jesus does not qualify or grant exceptions to this teaching, nor does the commandment not to murder (Exodus 20:13). In the Genesis creation myth, Adam and Eve are expelled from the garden for even *seeking the knowledge* of good and evil, lest they become like God (Genesis 3:5). The sorting of good and bad, righteous and evil, large fish from small ones, wheat from tares, and friend from enemy is the job of angels, not humans. Only God blesses and condemns the good and the evil, in a time we do not control or even know. Meanwhile, as we live our daily lives, we are to avoid both demonizing others, which leads to violence, and romanticizing or sentimentalizing others, which is a form of idolatry.

Questions for Discussion

1. *Do you think it is possible not to judge people? What about the language we use? Is it possible to show disapproval without labelling someone as "evil" or "bad"? How might we do this?*
2. *Name some consequences of separating "good" from "evil"? How can we know which is which?*
3. *Can there ever be a difference between a person's actions, and who they really are inside?*
4. *Can a "good" person ever commit an "evil" act? Can an "evil" person ever commit a "good" act?*
5. *What is the benefit of leaving the separation of good and evil to the "angels" at the end of the age?*

~ 25 ~

The Unforgiving Slave

WHAT DO YOU THINK?
Should we always forgive a debt, insult, or abuse; or should we always
demand full accountability? Or is there a third way?

Matthew 18:21–35

[21]Then Peter came and said to him, "Lord, if another member of the church sins against me, how often should I forgive? As many as seven times?" [22]Jesus said to him, "Not seven times, but, I tell you, seventy-seven times.

[23]"For this reason the kingdom of heaven may be compared to a king who wished to settle accounts with his slaves. [24]When he began the reckoning, one who owed him ten thousand talents was brought to him; [25]and, as he could not pay, his lord ordered him to be sold, together with his wife and children and all his possessions, and payment to be made. [26]So the slave fell on his knees before him, saying, 'Have patience with me, and I will pay you everything.' [27]And out of pity for him, the lord of that slave released him and forgave him the debt. [28]But that same slave, as he went out, came upon one of his fellow-slaves who owed him a hundred denarii; and seizing him by the throat, he said, 'Pay what you owe.' [29]Then his fellow-slave fell down and pleaded with him, 'Have patience with me, and I will pay you.' [30]But he refused; then he went and threw him into prison until he should pay the debt. [31]When his fellow-slaves saw what had happened, they were greatly distressed, and they went and reported to their lord all that had taken place. [32]Then his lord summoned him and said to him, 'You wicked slave! I forgave you all that debt because you pleaded with me. [33]Should you not have had mercy on your fellow-slave, as I had mercy on you?' [34]And in anger his lord handed him over to be tortured until he should pay his entire debt. [35]So my heavenly Father will also do to every one of you, if you do not forgive your brother or sister from your heart."

A New Vision

To represent this parable visually requires at least three scenes: the original forgiveness granted by the king, the unwillingness to forgive on the part of the slave, and finally, the scene that shows the consequences.

I imagine on the first side of a three-sided relief a kingly figure lifting a huge bag of money (shown in negative space to illustrate a lack of money or a debt) off the shoulders of a slave who is begging for debt relief.

The second scene shows that same slave trying to extract a debt from another slave by choking him.

A person in the background tries to remind him of the forgiveness of his own huge debt (represented by the same negative space in reverse on side two).

The third scene shows the consequences of failing to forgive one's debtors.

The bag of money falls back on the slave.

Combined, these scenes represent the two solutions with which Matthew frames the parable. We need to go back to Matthew 18:15–20 to find Jesus' third way.

Parable Research

This parable, found only in Matthew, goes to the heart of the dilemma of how we relate to other people and to God. Even though Peter asks a question about the sins of a church member, the parable can and often has been applied to *all* people. Also, in the parable, "sin" includes debt, insult, and abuse. Therefore, the parable is about owing and forgiving debt, which can be understood both as a monetary debt or as a spiritual debt incurred from an insult or abuse.

But the question remains: when one person owes another person a great debt or an apology or redress for an insult or abuse, how far does that person go to repay that debt, or to apologize for or redress the insult or abuse? And how far does the person who is owed the debt or the apology or the redress go to forgive the debtor or the one who has transgressed either by insult or abuse? The dilemma is complex and one that Matthew struggled with as he tried to interpret Jesus' parable.

Even though prior to this parable Matthew reports Jesus spelling out a four-step approach to solving conflicts (Matthew 18:15–20), here he gives only two answers to this dilemma: one before the parable and one after. First, he reports Jesus saying to Peter that we must forgive 77 times, or 70 times seven in some translations, which, practically speaking, is almost an infinite number and may have been *meant* to indicate infinite forgiveness. Neither Jesus nor Matthew allow for exceptions to this infinite forgiveness.

Next, Matthew reports the parable, in which a slave is forgiven a monumental debt of 10,000 talents – an amount estimated to equal about 100 million dollars. The king forgives this huge debt, but the slave then refuses to forgive the small debt that another slave owes him. When the king finds out about the first slave's lack of forgiveness, he angrily condemns him to torture until he pays up. Matthew adds that God will do the same to others who do not forgive.

So Matthew *does* make an exception to forgiveness. That exception is that we will *not* be forgiven when we do not forgive others. In other words,

Matthew seems to read Jesus as preaching unlimited forgiveness at first, but then also preaching punishment, even torture, for those who do not forgive. How can we untangle this dilemma?

The problem is universal and timeless. People have always sought to even the score of debt, whether the debt is money or insult or abuse. An eye for an eye and a tooth for a tooth was and still is taught as a way to "get even." The rule of revenge captivates whole nations and tribes and clans, so that wars often smoulder for centuries between rival groups. However, before we in North America get too righteous about chronic warfare in the Balkans, Northern Ireland, or the Middle East, the same dynamic permeates our own government policies, not to mention our television shows and movies, which often end with our celluloid heroes wreaking violent revenge against evildoers. The score is evened at last – or at least until the other side counters with more violence to even the score yet again. This is called the cycle of "redemptive violence," a phenomenon articulated and well analyzed by New Testament scholar Walter Wink (42–62).

The parable's ending, in which the king or God sends the unforgiving debtor to be tortured, lends itself to an interpretation that favours redemptive violence. The king's first act of mercy is consistent with Matthew's first report of Jesus' word to Peter: infinite forgiveness. It is also consistent with other sayings of Jesus in which forgiveness overcomes revenge and stops the cycle of violence. In Matthew 5:38–43 Jesus says,

> You have heard that it was said, "an eye for an eye and a tooth for a tooth." But I say to you, Do not resist an evildoer... You have heard that it was said, "You shall love your neighbour and hate your enemy." But I say to you, Love your enemies and pray for those who persecute you...

This kind of forgiveness is also part of the Lord's Prayer in which we ask forgiveness "as we forgive our debtors." But then, Matthew makes this one exception. When we ourselves do not forgive, then "always forgive" becomes "almost always." So for Matthew, it is unforgivable not to forgive.

Unfortunately, Matthew's argument has caused untold pain and grief to countless numbers of people over the centuries – particularly to women. For years, women have been told and pressured to forgive all manner of abuse. Worse, they've been made to feel that it is "unforgivable" for them *not* to do so. But should a spouse really forgive an abusive partner 77 times? Well, no. There are limits and boundaries. There must be consequences for one's abusive actions. And most of us would probably agree that justifiable debts *do* need to be paid. Obviously, we need a third way, a middle course between infinite forgiveness and redemptive violence.

This "third way" has been articulated and elaborated upon by many people who subscribe to non-violent schools of thought, and action, and ways of being. Note especially the work of Walter Wink, mentioned above.

In the third way, the debtor, insulter, or abuser is always confronted. But violence and revenge are avoided by following the four steps Matthew reports in 18:15–20. I call these four, progressive steps negotiation, mediation, arbitration, and "leavitation." More specifically, they involve 1.) one-on-one negotiation, "alone" as Jesus says in 18:15, 2.) third-party mediation, 3.) arbitration by a larger group, such as the whole church or civic body, and, finally, 4.) dismissal or moving beyond the debt, insult, or abuse and treating the other like a tax collector. (See my book *Resolving Conflict with Justice and Peace*.)

There is nothing esoteric about this third way. We use it in bankruptcy proceedings, for example, where debtors are allowed to repay debts according to plans negotiated and agreed to by both parties. Abuse and insults and even some property and other crimes can be and often are justly reconciled through restorative justice procedures. This third way has been used in labour/management disputes, international diplomacy, and even in schoolyard conflict resolution training.

In Matthew 18:15–20, Jesus shows us, on the one hand, how to confront debt, insult, and abuse without violence, and, on the other hand, how to avoid the kind of infinite forgiveness that amounts to surrender. In a word, a debt, insult, or case of abuse is changed from a score that must be "settled" or made "even," to a *problem to be solved* by all parties who are affected by it. Thus Matthew offers this third way even before he frames the parable with only two options.

As answers to debt, insult, or abuse, the two options Matthew presents in the parable –infinite forgiveness or torture for those who don't forgive – contradict each other. But maybe it is this very contradiction that will drive us to seek the third way of non-violent problem solving.

Questions for Discussion

1. *Name some of your experiences of debt forgiveness.*
2. *Name occasions where you forgave an insult or debt.*
3. *Where do you draw the line on forgiveness and on revenge?*
4. *Name cultural expressions of "redemptive violence."*
5. *Did Jesus seek revenge or forgive without any consequences?*
6. *How might the third way work in your own life?*

~ 26 ~

The Vineyard Workers

WHAT DO YOU THINK?
How do authorities blame the victim and then convince the victim that
they (the authorities) are generous?

Matthew 20:1–16

[1]For the kingdom of heaven is like a landowner who went out early in the morning to hire labourers for his vineyard. [2]After agreeing with the labourers for the usual daily wage, he sent them into his vineyard. [3]When he went out about nine o'clock, he saw others standing idle in the marketplace; [4]and he said to them, "You also go into the vineyard, and I will pay you whatever is right." So they went. [5]When he went out again about noon and about three o'clock, he did the same. [6]And about five o'clock he went out and found others standing around; and he said to them, "Why are you standing here idle all day?" [7]They said to him, "Because no one has hired us." He said to them, "You also go into the vineyard." [8]When evening came, the owner of the vineyard said to his manager, "Call the labourers and give them their pay, beginning with the last and then going to the first." [9]When those hired about five o'clock came, each of them received the usual daily wage. [10]Now when the first came, they thought they would receive more; but each of them also received the usual daily wage. [11]And when they received it, they grumbled against the landowner, [12]saying, "These last worked only one hour, and you have made them equal to us who have borne the burden of the day and the scorching heat." [13]But he replied to one of them, "Friend, I am doing you no wrong; did you not agree with me for the usual daily wage? [14]Take what belongs to you and go; I choose to give to this last the same as I give to you. [15]Am I not allowed to do what I choose with what belongs to me? Or are you envious because I am generous?" [16]So the last will be first, and the first will be last.

A New Vision

To imagine or illustrate this parable, we can focus on the final scene where the vineyard workers line up for their pay. Note that the landlord manipulates them by paying the last hired first. He is very large compared to the workers because of the power he has to determine everything in this situation.

The four workers' postures depict their attitudes. (There are five sets of workers in the parable but only four in the sculpture.) The last hired are happy to receive the one denarius for one hour of work, even though it is a pittance. The workers in the line up get progressively more resentful, until the last one raises his fist in anger.

The owner is confident, overbearing, and assertive as he offers the one coin from his bag of money.

This reading of the parable unmasks the unjust system in which the landowner has the power to manipulate the day labourers to accept his terms without debate. He contracts with the first hired for only one denarius, which amounts to one day of survival. For the rest he decides what *he* thinks is fair, and they have to accept it. Having virtually no power, they are forced in this system to accept whatever work they can get.

To picture the owner as dominant, arrogant, and stingy instead of as a gracious God figure is the beginning of liberation, because it unmasks the colonial ideology that blames the victim.

Parable Research

The parable of the vineyard workers is found only in Matthew and has almost always been interpreted with the landowner as God and the workers as ungrateful recipients of his generous decision to pay all the workers equally for their work in his vineyard. Matthew frames the parable with "The kingdom of heaven is like a landowner" (already suggesting that he is a God figure) and ends it with "the last will be first and the first last," (seeming to justify the order of payment of the workers).

However, there is another way to interpret this parable if, as a beginning point, we accept with most scholars that Matthew's interpretive frames are his own and are not likely the words of Jesus. It is possible to view the parable from the point of view of the day labourers and come out with a very different reading.

We are trying to see in this book what the parables look like when we read them in the context of the social, political, and economic world of Jesus' time and place, namely occupied Palestine; and from the viewpoint of Jesus' peasant audiences.

Within this first-century context, we have noted that day labourers were the poorest of the poor. They had no land to sustain them or their children. These poor families could no longer feed themselves; they were cast out on their own to find whatever work they could. As William Herzog says, "For them, as Thomas Hobbes noted, life was 'solitary, poor, nasty, brutish and short'" (*Subversive Speech*, 88).

At the same time, we can assume that the landowner is well-off because he owns a vineyard large enough to require many workers to pick its crop. This would have been a cash crop for export, as opposed to a food crop or subsistence product. The landowner needs workers, and he goes to the town to hire them five times. He begins to exploit the first-hired by locking them into a one-denarius wage for the day's work, a minimal survival wage. They apparently have no bargaining power to get any more, and they agree to what he offers. The landowner does not even promise the others hired later one denarius, but only what *he* judges to be "right." Again, they cannot complain. They need to work or they will starve. Finally, the last workers to be hired do not even get this promise of what is "right." The landowner merely orders them, "You also go into the vineyard" (v. 7).

The insults to the workers continue at the end of the standard 12-hour workday, when they line up for their pay. Contrary to custom, the landowner calls the last hired, who worked only one hour, to come forward to be paid first. The first-hired, who worked 12 hours, can see that the last hired are paid one denarius; therefore, they expect a more generous prorated wage for their longer hours of work. "They thought they would receive more" (v. 10). But, to their surprise, the landowner also gives the first hired only the one denarius. So they begin to grumble, saying, "These last worked only one hour, and you have made them equal to us who have borne the burden of the day and the scorching heat" (v. 12). Then the landowner pulls one aside and makes him an example, using the tactic of divide and conquer. Not knowing his name and not bothering to find out, he calls him "friend," a patronizing title of a superior to an inferior. He said,

> I am doing you no wrong; did you not agree with me for the usual daily wage? Take what belongs to you and go... Am I not allowed to do what I choose with what belongs to me? Or are you envious because I am generous? (vv. 14–16)

The landowner insists on his righteousness and generosity to the workers and reminds the first hired that they had agreed to his wage, even though they really had no choice. Then he claims total ownership of the whole enterprise and accuses the protesting worker of envy, thus blaming the victim.

From the workers' point of view, the landowner cannot be a figure for God, as usually interpreted, because he manipulated the powerless workers, arrogantly made all the decisions, insulted, and blamed them for envy, and then claimed his own generosity.

To be sure, this interpretation of the owner as a tyrant rather than as a symbol of God is not a consensus view. Bernard Brandon Scott sees the owner's acts as gracious gestures, as treating everyone equally, just as God treats everyone equally. He concludes his analysis of the parable by saying that the grace offered by the owner is not the equal wage or even equal justice, but the *invitation* to the kingdom, which is offered to all. Scott acknowledges that one denarius is hardly a generous wage, but that is not the point for him. Rather, *grace* is the point.

> Those commentators who see grace as the major theme of the parable are correct. The denarius, however, is not the metaphor of grace; rather, the need for workers, the call, is the metaphor (Footnote, 297).

Perhaps Scott's interpretation is correct, but it is not likely one that the workers would appreciate.

The view that the owner manipulates the poor workers, on the other hand, has the advantage of not assuming that God is an arbitrary oppressor who overwhelms these workers. These poor day labourers were similar to Jesus' closest followers. In other words, the peasant followers of Jesus were quite vulnerable. Herzog sums up their condition:

> Every peasant's plot of land was a reminder of Yahweh's covenant with the people. The land was invested with theological import. By contrast, the Romans and their Herodian clients viewed the land as an asset to be managed and a commodity to be exploited. For this reason, they were willing to foreclose on peasants who could not repay their loans and seize the land as a way of increasing their holdings.
>
> To justify their predatory behavior, the ruling class established an ideology that would mystify what was happening and blame the victims of their practices. Their ideology blamed the poor for their poverty, as though it were their sole responsibility, and mystified the system that rigged the economic game against them... (*Prophet*, 145–146).

If this interpretation from the worker's point of view is closer to Jesus' original message, why would Jesus tell such a parable when it is so discouraging?

The answer could be that he may have been teaching the oppressed workers to unmask the economic system that kept them in poverty, fatalism, and hopelessness. Even though these oppressed workers were "submerged" in a "culture of silence" (Freier), they began to speak up. They "grumbled" and thus made the first step of protest.

The parable ends here, but a next step would be to counter the tactics of the owner by organizing the other workers, so that together they might have some small power to resist the landowner's manipulations.

Questions for Discussion

1. *Do you think the landowner is generous or manipulative?*
2. *Are the workers lazy, ungrateful, or right to protest their pay?*
3. *Name a similar labour-management dispute today.*
4. *Is there any hope in this parable?*

~ 27 ~

The Two Children

WHAT DO YOU THINK?
Which is most important: talking or doing?

[22]"Whatever you ask for in prayer with faith, you will receive."

[23]When he entered the temple, the chief priests and the elders of the people came to him as he was teaching, and said, "By what authority are you doing these things, and who gave you this authority?" [24]Jesus said to them, "I will also ask you one question; if you tell me the answer, then I will also tell you by what authority I do these things. [25]Did the baptism of John come from heaven, or was it of human origin?" And they argued with one another, "If we say, 'From heaven,' he will say to us, 'Why then did you not believe him?' [26]But if we say, 'Of human origin,' we are afraid of the crowd; for all regard John as a prophet." [27]So they answered Jesus, "We do not know." And he said to them, "Neither will I tell you by what authority I am doing these things.

[28]"What do you think? A man had two sons; he went to the first and said, 'Son, go and work in the vineyard today.' [29]He answered, 'I will not'; but later he changed his mind and went. [30]The father went to the second and said the same; and he answered, 'I go, sir'; but he did not go. [31]Which of the two did the will of his father?" They said, "The first." Jesus said to them, "Truly I tell you, the tax-collectors and the prostitutes are going into the kingdom of God ahead of you. [32]For John came to you in the way of righteousness and you did not believe him, but the tax-collectors and the prostitutes believed him; and even after you saw it, you did not change your minds and believe him."

A New Image

What images can we create to represent this parable? The two children's responses suggest two scenes.

One scene depicts an eager son agreeing to work in the vineyard, running toward the baskets he'll gather the grapes in. Three images of the son in perspective simulate this eagerness to work, as he rushes forward to volunteer. A second child is lying down and is saying "no" with a hand signal. She seems determined to stay at her leisure. I have used a female figure to shift the usual translation from "sons" to "children."

The second scene reverses the roles, as in the parable. The son who eagerly agreed to work lies down at his ease. But the child who said "no" walks back to work. She is represented as three figures in perspective, to simulate the distance to the vineyard at the top of the relief sculpture. The figures of the no-sayer grow smaller as she goes off to work in the distant vineyard.

Parable Research

On one level, this parable, which only appears in Matthew, is relatively straightforward. It is about being reliable and doing what you say you will do. However, on another level it is also about Jesus' authority, and about the verbal debates that Jesus' opponents used to challenge him and his message about God's Empire.

First, we need to look at the honour/shame context of verbal debates in Jesus' day, to see how important this exchange really is. In a critical study entitled *The Social World of Luke-Acts*, Jerome Neyrey and Bruce Malina have co-authored a chapter that spells out the sophisticated aspects of the honour debates Jesus had with the authorities. Jesus usually won these debates, as reported in Matthew and in the other gospels. Each win increased his honour and authority, resulting in the development and growth of his large following. Had he lost the debates, his honour and authority would have diminished, as would have the number of his followers.

I will apply Malina's and Neyrey's schema, which describes how honour debates function, to this parable and its context. This debate schema is made up of the following parts: claim, challenge, riposte, and verdict (50–51).

To see the full context of the debate, we have to back up in the text to the point where Jesus begins the process by making a *claim* – or two of them, in fact. On the previous day, Jesus had visited the Temple. While there, he had overturned the tables of the moneychangers, and had accused them of making the Temple, which should have been a house of prayer, into a den of robbers (21:13). That was his first claim. The next day, the day of debate, he is once again back in the Temple teaching, when he makes his second claim: "Whatever you ask for in prayer, you will receive" (21:22). In other words, prayer works.

These claims are then *challenged* by the authorities, because Jesus had no obvious standing with them. They say to him, "By what authority are you doing these things and who gave you this authority?" (v. 23). This challenge represents the second step in the honour/authority debate.

The third step is Jesus' *riposte*, which consists of a question and then the parable. First, he asks the authorities where John's baptism came from – was it from heaven or was it of human origin. He promises to answer their question after they answer his. Their answer (after a huddle noting that either answer will trap them) is a vague, "We do not know." They dodge Jesus' question.

Because they won't answer his question, Jesus says he will not answer *their* question, but he then keeps them on the defensive by asking another question and telling a parable: "What do you think? A man has two children…" (usually translated "sons," but the Greek *teknon* means child not *huios,* meaning son). The first child says "no" to the father's command to work in the vineyard, but later goes to work. The second says "yes" and then does nothing.

Jesus' second riposte is, "Which child did the work of the father?" When the chief priests and elders answer, "the first," he springs the trap saying, "tax collectors and prostitutes are going into the kingdom of God ahead of you," for they believed John, who was righteous, "yet you did not believe him…and even after you saw it you did not change your minds and believe him." Presumably, the priests and elders were like the second child who *says* he will follow the way of righteousness, but then *does* nothing. By their own answer they condemn themselves, because they said the first child did the will of God. By rewarding the no-sayer-but-doer with righteousness, they condemn themselves because they are like the yes-sayer who does nothing.

The parable and the story end here, but the assumption is that Jesus won the debate and thus the *verdict*, the final stage in the honour/authority debate schema.

This parable fits well with many other exchanges Jesus had with the religious authorities. These authorities are the ones who followed the ideology of the purity codes, which were used to keep the poor down, while the urban elites, Roman taxation, and the military forces kept them under control. This ideology claimed that the status quo was God's will and that the peasants needed to obey the authorities and never question them. It also sought to justify the Roman conquerors and their local collaborators, who claimed to be righteous and to care for and help the people, but who did the opposite.

Matthew reports another metaphor and parable that says "do what you say" and "practice what you preach," in his seventh chapter. There Jesus uses the metaphor of a tree that bears the good fruit of good works (7:17). It is not a matter of only hearing Jesus' words; we must *act* on them. This action is illustrated in the parable of the two builders (7:24–27), which we discussed in chapter 20. We must build our lives on the solid foundation of good deeds, not on the shaky pillars of an ideology that justifies the status quo of oppression.

We find another example of the imperative of doing deeds in Matthew 23, where Jesus says that the words of the scribes and the Pharisees who sit on Moses' seat are good teachings that all should follow. But these authorities do not do as they say, for "they do not practice what they teach. They tie up heavy burdens, hard to bear, and lay them on the shoulders of others; but they themselves are unwilling to lift a finger to move them" (vv. 2–4). Jesus calls these Pharisees and scribes "hypocrites," who burden others but claim to be righteous themselves.

In our time, we also have religious figures who claim to be righteous, yet they limit morality to private, family, and reproductive issues, while they ignore or support war-making, ruthless money-making, and oppose government poverty programs. They focus on winning "converts to Christ." This privatized Christianity does just what Jesus charges the authorities with doing, "For you cross sea and land to make a single convert, and you make the new convert twice as much a child of hell as yourselves" (23:15).

The parables can be used to "convert" people by ignoring the political and economic world in Jesus' time and in our time. However, if we look at the parable and the other honour debates in their social, economic, and political context, we see that the "burden" the authorities were putting on the peasants consisted literally of the debts and the oppression that kept them poor and that overwhelmed them as they simply sought to survive.

That economic and political burden must have been part of what Jesus was getting at in the challenges he made to the authorities who kept the status quo. This is why "great crowds followed [Jesus] from Galilee, the Decapolis, Jerusalem, Judea, and from beyond the Jordan" (Matthew 4:25). And it was why these corrupt authorities supported Rome's crucifixion of him. They did not like the fact that Jesus unmasked their ideology of oppression. So they killed him.

Questions for Discussion

1. *Few doubt that the crowds followed Jesus because he healed people. Do you agree that his ability to debate might also have attracted a following?*

2. *If Jesus were here today, which religious and secular authorities do you think he would engage in debate?*

3. *Using this parable, Jesus accuses the priests and elders of only saying they follow the way of righteousness, when in fact they don't follow it at all. What do you think Jesus would say about us? Why?*

4. *How did Jesus support the Hebrew tradition yet challenge the keepers of that tradition?*

~ 28 ~

The Young Women

WHAT DO YOU THINK?
Are you ready for God's Empire of non-violence, peace, and justice?

Matthew 25:1–13

[1]Then the kingdom of heaven will be like this. Ten bridesmaids took their lamps and went to meet the bridegroom. [2]Five of them were foolish, and five were wise. [3]When the foolish took their lamps, they took no oil with them; [4]but the wise took flasks of oil with their lamps. [5]As the bridegroom was delayed, all of them became drowsy and slept. [6]But at midnight there was a shout, "Look! Here is the bridegroom! Come out to meet him." [7]Then all those bridesmaids got up and trimmed their lamps. [8]The foolish said to the wise, "Give us some of your oil, for our lamps are going out." [9]But the wise replied, "No! there will not be enough for you and for us; you had better go to the dealers and buy some for yourselves." [10]And while they went to buy it, the bridegroom came, and those who were ready went with him into the wedding banquet; and the door was shut. [11]Later the other bridesmaids came also, saying, "Lord, lord, open to us." [12]But he replied, "Truly I tell you, I do not know you." [13]Keep awake therefore for you know neither the day nor the hour.

A New Image

What images can we create to represent this parable? Again, a two-sided relief seems appropriate to represent the inclusion of five young women and the exclusion of the other five. The ones left out with empty lamps are not happy.

They line up outside the residence of the wedding party, crying to get in. But the door is closed.

This is side one of the relief.

On the second side, the other women whose lamps were ready are enjoying the wedding party. They are line dancing, some holding their burning lamps.

Does this inside/outside picture mean that we must interpret the parable as having an exclusionary message, which seems contrary to the egalitarian message of Jesus?

Perhaps the unready women will be excluded from God's Empire, but the invitation is always there. I have represented this choice by having the door closed, but unlocked. There are consequences for not being ready, but God is still a God of love, who welcomes all to the banquet, the symbol of God's Empire.

Parable Research

This parable of the young women goes by many names: The Ten Virgins, The Ten Bridesmaids, The Maidens, The Closed Door, or simply The Young Women. The latter name seems less offensive to me than some of the others. It also communicates that the women in the parable are probably quite young, for marriages in Jesus' time were arranged for young women in their early teens, and wedding parties included marriageable young women, such as these ten.

This parable is unique to Matthew, although Luke also records a type of closed door for anyone who is not ready (13:22–30). The Young Women parable fits into Matthew's apocalyptic warnings, along with the parables of the Talents, the Doorkeepers and the Overseer, and the Last Judgement. In these parables, those who practise good deeds (nourishing the hungry and the thirsty, clothing the naked, and visiting the sick and the imprisoned) are taken in. Those who do not are excluded. In this case of the young women, they are preparing for a wedding celebration, to which the groom is due to take them.

The lamps, whether lit or not, make little sense literally and may be taken as symbols for doing God's word. Barbara Reid (*Mark, Year A*, 194–196) points out that a lit lamp in the Bible is a symbol for good deeds: being a "light to the world," "a lamp unto my feet" (Psalm 119:105); not hiding one's lamp "under the bushel basket" (Mark 4:21). Thus, the young women who have their lamps ready, with enough oil to burn to light their way, symbolize being ready with good deeds for the Day of Judgement and the return of the Christ.

Matthew's inclusion of Jesus' parable can be read as an urgent plea for discipline directed at a very threatened, tiny Jewish sect in about 85 CE, after Rome crushed the Jewish rebellion and destroyed the Temple in Jerusalem in 70 CE. Matthew uses the fear of exclusion to emphasize the need for vigilance in doing good deeds, a point he makes throughout his gospel. Here, the five young women who were lax in keeping their lamps ready are left out of the wedding celebration. The door is closed; the groom does not know them.

Compare this exclusion with Jesus' teaching in the Sermon on the Mountain, where he says, "Knock and the door will be opened" (Matthew 7:7). The young women in this parable did knock, without such welcome results. Also, compare this exclusion to Matthew's frequent references to torture and to being "thrown into outer darkness," where "there is crying and grinding of teeth," for not following the way of love, inclusion, and forgiveness that Jesus taught (Matthew 8:12, 13:42, 13:50, 22:13, 24:51, 25:30). These references represent an obvious internal contradiction in the gospel, because Matthew elsewhere reports Jesus preaching a God of love and of near infinite forgiveness (Matthew 18:22).

Scholars point out that Matthew was dealing with a frightened community, which had been waiting for the return of Jesus for decades, in the midst of an oppressive Roman occupation. So Matthew's interpretations of Jesus' parables tilt toward the needs of that early community. And part of that need was for alertness and readiness – displayed by doing good deeds, and by actively serving those in need. Thus, like the young women with extra oil for their lamps, they are poised for Jesus' imminent return. This is Matthew's agenda and it is followed aggressively by many today who stress an end-of-the world theology. Fear of punishment *does* motivate us to a degree.

However, many scholars suggest that this parable is solely a construction of the early church and not from Jesus at all. Perhaps there is a core story attributable to him, but the locked door and the words of the groom about not knowing the five young women left outside are not consistent with the other teachings of Jesus. Jesus taught inclusion, not exclusion; love, not punishment; and forgiveness, not holy revenge. Is there a third way? Some scholars point out that in Luke's version of the Feast or Great Supper parable, those who are not prepared simply miss the food at the party (Luke 14:24), while Matthew has them thrown into outer darkness (Matthew 22:2–13).

Since Luke and the other gospels have different ways of reporting Jesus' words and deeds, whom do we believe? Which version of judgement do we affirm: the inclusive or exclusive version? The overwhelming number of stories in which Jesus emphasizes inclusion seems to argue for the inclusive version of judgement as well. But perhaps the reality that we are accountable for our actions argues for the exclusive version.

I lean towards a third option, in which the offer to come and join Jesus' way is given. We can reject the offer, and there are consequences for doing so, but they are not punishments; they are the self-chosen consequences of our choices. The five young women who have prepared for the way of goodness – by doing active deeds of goodness – get to celebrate and let their light shine. The five young women who are not prepared for the way of goodness are not punished, but they *do* face the consequences. They do not get to celebrate. That is all. Their judgement is self-chosen, a third way.

Questions for Discussion

1. *Are the young women who refuse to share their oil not being charitable – refusing to do a good deed? Yet they are rewarded anyway. What do you think?*
2. *How do we explain the different interpretations of Jesus' parables within the various gospels?*
3. *If Jesus taught inclusion, how do we have accountability, for example, in a situation of spouse abuse?*
4. *If Jesus taught exclusion, how do we square that with his statement that we must forgive 70 times seven?*

~ 29 ~

The Talents

WHAT DO YOU THINK?
When the rich exploit the work of the poor, what can we do about it?

Matthew 25:14–30

[14]For it is as if a man, going on a journey, summoned his slaves and entrusted his property to them; [15]to one he gave five talents, to another two, to another one, to each according to his ability. Then he went away. [16]The one who had received the five talents went off at once and traded with them, and made five more talents. [17]In the same way, the one who had the two talents made two more talents. [18]But the one who had received the one talent went off and dug a hole in the ground and hid his master's money. [19]After a long time the master of those slaves came and settled accounts with them. [20]Then the one who had received the five talents came forward, bringing five more talents, saying, "Master, you handed over to me five talents; see, I have made five more talents." [21]His master said to him, "Well done, good and trustworthy slave; you have been trustworthy in a few things, I will put you in charge of many things; enter into the joy of your master." [22]And the one with the two talents also came forward, saying, "Master, you handed over to me two talents; see, I have made two more talents." [23]His master said to him, "Well done, good and trustworthy slave; you have been trustworthy in a few things, I will put you in charge of many things; enter into the joy of your master." [24]Then the one who had received the one talent also came forward, saying, "Master, I knew that you were a harsh man, reaping where you did not sow, and gathering where you did not scatter seed; [25]so I was afraid, and I went and hid your talent in the ground. Here you have what is yours." [26]But his master replied, "You wicked and lazy slave! You knew, did you, that I reap where I did not sow, and gather where I did not scatter? [27]Then you ought to have invested my money with the bankers, and on my return I would have received what was my own with interest. [28]So take the talent from him, and give it to the one with the ten talents. [29]For to all those who have, more will be given, and they will have an abundance; but from those who have nothing, even what they have will be taken away. [30]As for this worthless slave, throw him into the outer darkness, where there will be weeping and gnashing of teeth."

(See also Luke 19:12–27, and Eusebius on the Gospel of the Nazoreans.)

A New Image

What images come to mind with this parable? I see a two-sided relief. The first side of the relief depicts the parable as Jesus tells it in Matthew. A harsh master commands slaves to help him in his usury.

Rather than work himself, he lives off the labour of others. The two slaves have invested the money, shown in bags, while the third has buried his. In the relief, the first two slaves are bringing back the profits they have made on the invested money. All of this business is going on within the context of a country conquered and occupied by the Roman empire. I have symbolized this political context by framing the scene with Roman soldiers. The third slave who buried the money is condemned. He sits over the spot where the money lies.

The second side of the relief shows what *could* happen, if God's Empire was actually lived out. The master returns to collect the profits from the slaves. Two of them make him more money, but the one who hides the money makes none.

However, when the accounts are called for, the third slave dares to challenge both the master's harshness and the fairness of the whole system. He risks his life in such a challenge, as depicted by the lowered swords of the Roman soldiers. The third slave expresses courage and the whole corrupt system is exposed and rejected.

Parable Research

Matthew's version of this parable is commonly called The Talents. Luke's version is usually called The Pounds. They are similar to each other, but there is no scholarly consensus about the relationship between them. I will focus on Matthew's version and on three ways to interpret the parable: literally, metaphorically, and politically.

The literal interpretation of this parable is often used in church stewardship drives and in sermons on giving, as well as in inspirational speeches at business luncheons. In these contexts, the parable is used to endorse capital investment and the making of money with money. Such an approach seems simple, clear, and obvious. However, this literal interpretation appears inconsistent with Jesus' life and message, and with other teachings elsewhere in the Bible. In the Hebrew Bible, such capital gain is called "usury" and is forbidden in Leviticus 25:36, Exodus 22:25, and Deuteronomy 23:19. Then, there is the problem of the violence against the third slave, who hides the talents. It requires an enormous stretch to image Jesus labelling someone as a "worthless slave" and then condemning that person "to the outer darkness where there will be weeping and gnashing of teeth" (v. 30).

A second, non-literal interpretation seems to be more consistent with the larger message of Jesus and to take better account of the context or placement of the parable within Matthew's gospel. I will call this the metaphorical interpretation. In this interpretation, the talents or pounds are seen metaphorically as spiritual gifts of the sort referred to in Romans 12, 1 Corinthians 12, and 1 Peter 4:10, where it says, "serve one another with whatever gift each...has received" (Hultgren, 271–291). That is, we have gifts (talents) of love, hope, faith, generosity, service, and care for the sick, hungry, and prisoners, all of which we are to use for God's realm. Both Matthew and Luke warn us to invest these gifts until Jesus returns and God's Empire comes to full fruition – *or else!*

Matthew makes the *or else* sentiment abundantly clear in the judgement portion of the parable, which I believe is a later addition to the parable made by Matthew. To understand why Matthew includes this, it's helpful to take note of the placement of the parable itself. Matthew situates this parable between the parable of the young women and the parable of the last judgement. As we have seen, the parable of the young women is about the need to be ready for the return of the Master, or Jesus. According to Matthew, the faith community should demonstrate this readiness by doing good works, by "investing" or using the talents or spiritual gifts they have been given. Clearly, in a time of great stress, when the community was under Roman occupation and when Jesus had failed to return as expected, Matthew used fear as a way to motivate his community to remain faithful.

Most scholars reject the literal interpretation, which endorses capital gain and usury, and follow instead this metaphorical interpretation, which promotes investing or using our spiritual gifts.

While the word talents *(talanton* in Greek) is thus sometimes interpreted metaphorically as an ability, skill, or gift, which we must invest wisely, it is worth noting that it is not used in this way in the Bible. In the Bible, the word *talanton* (or, in the case of Luke's "pounds," *mina*) refers only to money or weight and, in the parable, a very great deal of it. The value of a talent varied, but one estimate is that a single talent was worth 30 years of labour, and five talents were equal to 150 years of labour. As for Luke's pounds, they were less valuable, but still a large trust. One pound equalled 1,000 days of labour.

So where does that leave us?

If we take into account the social, economic, and political context in which the parable was told, a third interpretation presents itself. It is important here to pay some attention to the rich master, whose character is often overlooked while much discussion is given to the three slaves. The picture Jesus paints of the rich master is not at all flattering. He is called "harsh" and is described as one "who reaps where he did not sow and gathers where he did not scatter" (vv. 24, 26). These negative traits are first stated by the third slave, but the master does not object and in fact confirms the slave's assessment. In a word, he is cruel and vindictive; he lives off the work of others and abuses them without mercy when they do not do his bidding.

When we focus on the slave master in this way, the literal and metaphorical interpretations run into problems – serious problems. If the slave master is a symbol for God, then what kind of God are we left with? Certainly not the one Jesus describes in other parts of the gospels. Very few, if any, of us view God in this way.

Likewise, given the social, economic, and political context, it is highly unlikely that Jesus' audience, who were mostly peasants, would ever have identified the slave owner as God. In this scenario, Jesus would have told the parable as a way of exposing and opposing the whole domination system, which relied on slavery, usury, and the exploitation of the peasants. This political interpretation seems reasonable, since we know that Jesus said more about poverty and the well-being of social outcasts than just about anything else. We also know that he challenged the rich and the powerful over and over, calling them hypocrites and worse. We know he aimed his healing and love at "sinners," lepers, tax collectors, and prostitutes. We know he preached God's Empire of non-violent goodness, where fears and tears are overcome. Indeed, contrary to using fear and threats as Matthew and Luke do, Jesus said over and over, "Why are you afraid?" and "Do not fear" (Mark 4:40, 5:36).

With this political interpretation, we do not need the literal or the metaphorical interpretations. Nor do we have to be as hard on the timid slave as Matthew and Luke are. We are not tempted, for example, to assume that the master is a symbol for God or to go along with an interpretation that would have God say of his enemies, "bring them here and slaughter them in my presence" (Luke 19:27). We do not have to accept the revenge in Matthew against the "worthless slave" (v. 30). Such harsh judgements do not sound like Jesus, who said "love your enemies" (Luke 6:27).

Having said that, I am not sure I would go as far as William Herzog, who says that the third, timid slave is actually the hero of the parable and that Jesus was really describing how corrupt the system was (*Subversive Speech*, 150–168). That is, the third slave who hid the talents was doing the righteous thing by taking it out of the corrupt system of usurious exploitation. But these observations are worth considering and help us interpret the parable in a way that is more in line with Jesus' other teachings about a loving God who forgives sinners and seeks justice for slaves and other oppressed people.

So we have choices: the literal interpretation of investing capital for interest; the metaphorical interpretation of talents as spiritual gifts to be used, not hidden; or the political interpretation, which focuses on the master's harshness and on the system of usury that exploited the slaves.

Recently, scholars have drawn attention to the writings of Eusebius (260–340 CE), which mention a "Gospel of the Nazoreans," also from the second or third century CE. Eusebius reports that this gospel, which itself has never been found, contains a similar but also different version of this parable, one that has more in common with the political interpretation. In this extra-canonical writing, the first slave squanders his trusted money, the second makes some interest and is let off with a rebuke, but the third, who hid the money, is affirmed (Reid, *Matthew*, 208).

Obviously, no one can claim absolute certainty about the meaning of the parable. Indeed, the more one studies it, the more questions it raises. But, clearly, the literal approach makes no sense. The parable is a fantastic story about colossal piles of money that no one would leave to slaves to invest. The metaphorical approach, while attractive on some levels, still presents us with a cruel God and a reward/punishment ethic, which Jesus opposed. The political interpretation answers some of our questions, but not all of them. But that is what parables are like – they raise questions that require us to ponder their meaning and our faith.

Questions for Discussion

1. *Is it okay to question the editorial work of Matthew and Luke?*
2. *Which interpretation of this parable do you prefer: the literal, metaphorical, or political interpretation? Why?*
3. *Which one do you think Jesus would prefer? Why?*
4. *Do you think the various interpretations are mutually exclusive? Do we have to choose between meanings, or can the parable communicate different messages at different times and in different contexts?*
5. *How might we apply this parable to our own lives today?*

~ 30 ~

The Last Judgement

WHAT DO YOU THINK?
Who are "the least of these" in our time?

Matthew 25:31–46

[31]When the Son of Man comes in his glory, and all the angels with him, then he will sit on the throne of his glory. [32]All the nations will be gathered before him, and he will separate people one from another as a shepherd separates the sheep from the goats, [33]and he will put the sheep at his right hand and the goats at the left. [34]Then the king will say to those at his right hand, "Come, you that are blessed by my Father, inherit the kingdom prepared for you from the foundation of the world; [35]for I was hungry and you gave me food, I was thirsty and you gave me something to drink, I was a stranger and you welcomed me, [36]I was naked and you gave me clothing, I was sick and you took care of me, I was in prison and you visited me." [37]Then the righteous will answer him, "Lord, when was it that we saw you hungry and gave you food, or thirsty and gave you something to drink? [38]And when was it that we saw you a stranger and welcomed you, or naked and gave you clothing? [39]And when was it that we saw you sick or in prison and visited you?" [40]And the king will answer them, "Truly I tell you, just as you did it to one of the least of these who are members of my family, you did it to me." [41]Then he will say to those at his left hand, "You that are accursed, depart from me into the eternal fire prepared for the devil and his angels; [42]for I was hungry and you gave me no food, I was thirsty and you gave me nothing to drink, [43]I was a stranger and you did not welcome me, naked and you did not give me clothing, sick and in prison and you did not visit me." [44]Then they also will answer, "Lord, when was it that we saw you hungry or thirsty or a stranger or naked or sick or in prison, and did not take care of you?" [45]Then he will answer them, "Truly I tell you, just as you did not do it to one of the least of these, you did not do it to me." [46]And these will go away into eternal punishment, but the righteous into eternal life.

(See also Ezekiel 34:17–31.)

A New Image

Creating a fresh image of this parable was quite a challenge given that we have so many powerful scenes of the last judgement in Western art. Somehow, my new image needed to connect with a large number of other images: sheep, goats, and shepherd; the least; the nations; every person; Christ, and Christ within the least; and the separation of the goats and the sheep to the left and to the right. Also, it had to symbolize help for "the least of these." Yet I didn't want this "help" to be limited to charity, but to suggest political change as well – a tall order. Finally, I decided on a two-sided relief sculpture showing scattered sheep and goats, and a shepherd with a staff.

At the bottom centre of the image, we see the back of an average person, an "every person," on a road. This person refuses to respond to the hands, which extend from the left margin asking for help. These hands represent "the least."

On the second side of the relief, sheep and goats have been separated right and left. "The least" have emerged from the left side into the picture, with stigmata on their hands suggesting the presence of Christ in our midst.

These people are praying, feeding, drinking, protesting, leaning on a cane, and demanding justice. On the left side, the "every person" exits out of the goats' side of the picture. A new "every person" appears holding a basket containing food, drink, and clothing, to serve the charitable needs of the "least," but also raising a fist of political protest.

The shepherd on side one is replaced on side two by a torture victim in a cruciform posture. This makes the crucified Jesus a modern figure who is judging us from a modern cross of state terrorism.

Parable Research

Judgement day is a powerful image made painfully vivid in many paintings, especially Michelangelo's "Last Judgement" in the Sistine Chapel in Rome. The image of the afterlife, in which souls descend to hell or ascend to heaven, with Christ judging who goes where, sits deep in the psyche of Western minds. Michelangelo's image and many others are based on this apocalyptic parable found only in Matthew. Because of this image, it is hard for any of us in Christendom not to wonder, "Will I make the cut?"

The parable begins, like others, with an everyday simile, this time of a shepherd separating sheep and goats. This was a common practice in Jesus' time, which allowed for the protection and shearing of the more valuable sheep, and for the milking of the goats. Ezekiel has a similar judgement of God's "flock" (Ezekiel 34:17) and Matthew's parable is probably a variation built on it.

Yet Matthew's text may not be a parable at all. That question is the focus of one of four key debates that continue around this end-time picture in Matthew. Before we unravel these debates, however, it is helpful to understand the point of view of the text, which is an afterlife scene in which people are held accountable, as they are in the parable of The Rich Man and Lazarus. The narrator, like Emily in *Our Town*, tells the story from beyond the grave, as a warning to those still alive about how to behave here and now on earth. This God's-eye-view reflects back to us the norms by which God will judge us on judgement day, according to this parable. Like a course syllabus in college, it says, "Do this and you will pass; don't, and you won't."

John Donahue says that the "apocalyptic [point of view] is a view of history and human life from God's side" (119). He also sees it as a solution to theodicy, the question of why the innocent suffer and the unjust prosper, referred to in chapter 1 and the study of the Barren Fig Tree parable. The solution, on judgement day, reverses these accounts of rewards and punishments in this life. In other words, in the afterlife, justice finally wins out: the just prosper while the unjust suffer.

Now let's consider the four key debates or questions I mentioned above: 1.) Is this a parable, an allegory, or what? 2.) Is it authentically from Jesus or is it Matthew's invention? 3.) Who are "the least" among us (*anthropos*): all people or only Christians? and finally, 4.) Who are the "nations" (*ethne*), and are they saved or damned? Let's take these questions in order.

Is this a parable? Scholars are almost evenly divided on this question. Rudolf Bultmann calls it "an apocalyptic prediction" (*History*, 120–124). Geraint Vaughan Jones notes the allegorical elements of goats (the cursed), sheep (the blessed), and Son of Man (Jesus). However, the terms "Son of Man," "king," and "judge" are confused in this parable. Jones concludes that Matthew's text is a borderline case, yet he comes down on the side of calling it a parable rather than an allegory (106). A. T. Cadoux calls it a "semi-parable" (236), and John Donahue calls it an "apocalyptic parable" (110). Arland Hultgren says it is "an apocalyptic discourse with parabolic elements" (310).

Of all these judgements, John Donahue's assessment that it is an "apocalyptic parable" seems most reasonable to me, because the text has the necessary concrete comparison, a narrative movement, and the surprise twist at the end, which is the discovery of Christ in "the least of these." Yet it is also a special kind of narrative movement, in which both the beginning and the end occur beyond the earthly realm, making it apocalyptic.

Is this parable from Jesus or from Matthew? No one doubts that Matthew's fingerprints are all over it. It expresses his strong ethical stance, which requires that we move beyond talk of faith to actual *deeds* of love done for the afflicted. Harsh punishment awaits those who do not care for the afflicted. Joachim Jeremias notes that the parable contains a number of references to Jesus, both in terms of how he is named and the role he plays, that would only have been used after Jesus' death: for example, the Son of Man is named "king," and serves as "judge" (143). This parable also fits with Matthew's apocalyptic discourse, in which persecution, false prophets, and signs of the end times are presented along with the end-time parables – The Door Keepers and the Overseer, The Young Women, and The Talents – immediately before The Last Judgement.

These aspects and others lead Robert Funk and the Jesus Seminar to rule it definitely not from Jesus. However, Arland Hultgren says Jesus' authorship is "probable" (326), and Joachim Jeremias, quoting T. W. Manson (*Sayings*), concludes that although it is not authentic in detail, we must credit it to Jesus for its "startling originality," by which he means the "startling surprise" of the Messiah hidden in "the least of these."

From my own perspective, I am struck by the incongruity of having Jesus – whom we find in the hungry, thirsty, homeless, naked, sick, and imprisoned – suddenly elevated to the position of royal judge presiding over the court of last resort. If I take the harsh condemnation as typical of Matthew and the later references to Christ as "king" and "judge" as the early church speaking, and combine these with the incongruity named above, I am left tilting towards the view that Matthew is the author, but that he probably built this parable on an earlier saying of Jesus.

Who are "the least of these"? Jesus insists that his followers do deeds of love for the least, rather for himself, when he asks, "Why do you call me 'Lord, Lord,' and do not *do* what I tell you?" (Luke 6:46 followed by The Two Builders parable. See also Matthew 7:21.) Yet some scholars believe that "the least" refers only to Christian missionaries. These missionaries, like Paul, must be cared for as they make their mendicant journeys. Other scholars insist that this is a narrow sectarian view, which limits good deeds of caring to other Christians and which is contrary to Jesus, who says, "If you love those who love you, what credit is that to you?" (Luke 6:32).

John Donahue attempts a mid-course denying "sectarianism" but saying that "the least" are principally not the afflicted but the "church in mission" (123). His solution is not convincing for a number of reasons. Arland Hultgren points out that "the six misfortunes [hunger, thirst, etc.] do not begin to coincide with the activities of the persecutors in this Gospel, namely slandering, killing, and flogging of the disciples" (323). Also, nothing in the list of the six afflictions characterizes missionaries alone. They apply to all people. Comparable lists of the afflicted are found in the Hebrew Bible, in ancient Egypt, and in rabbinical literature.

It seems obvious to me that "the least" refers to *all* people, no matter what their religion, who hunger or thirst or languish in prison; who are homeless, naked, or sick.

Who are "the nations" (ethne) being judged? Does "the nations" include the Gentiles (leaving out the Jews and non-believers) or does it refer to all people? Joachim Jeremias calls the non-believers "heathen," but argues that they are also justified "on the ground of love" (145). The justified are those who care for the afflicted. They, not only Christians, are saved from hell and are blessed like the sheep at the right hand of God. Arland Hultgren sees "all humanity" as awaiting judgement (313). The norm is behaviour, not belief. David Buttrick makes this inclusiveness quite welcoming: "Could a happy humanist make the grade? Why not...?" (126).

But all these who are included, which is to say all people who do or do not declare allegiance to Christ, still have a big job, not only to avoid evil, not only to see and to talk about the afflictions of people, but to actually *do* the deeds of love needed by the afflicted. As Jeremias says, "guilt does not lie in the commission of gross sins, but in the omission of good deeds" (143).

The ancient theological debate about grace versus works is present in this parable. That is, the great paradox of justification by grace combined with the necessity to do works of mercy is clarified here. Rudolph Bultmann sums up this central Christian theme of faith and works focused so vividly in the parable. The "judgment of the Lord does not depend upon your conscious confession of faith, but on the faith which is working unconsciously in your behaviour" (Hultgren, 327, from a sermon by Bultmann).

For myself, this scene of the last judgement in Matthew corrects the order of the fundamentalists' "crusades for Christ," in which confessions of belief take priority over deeds of love for the afflicted. The final justice here rewards the good and holds the evil accountable *before* they even know Christ is present in the afflicted, and even whether or not they confess Christ in words. One does not confess Christ and then do some good when one gets around to it... later... maybe. One does good by serving the least and the afflicted, then finds the Christ in the very ones served.

1. How do you imagine judgement day?
2. Do you believe that some will be blessed and others cursed?
3. The parable says that "the nations" will be brought before God to be judged, at which time the good will be separated from the bad. Do you believe this includes non-Christians as well as Christians? Do you think God blesses "good" non-Christians? Why or why not?
4. Who are the least today and how can we serve them?
5. How do we move beyond charity?

Conclusion

My four-year journey through the parables has convinced me that the wisdom they contain is still rich and critically valuable for those of us who seek the way of Jesus. Just as Mark, Matthew, Luke, and Thomas applied the parables of Jesus to the needs of their day, we can apply them to the needs of our time.

The first step in this journey has been to learn, from the relevant scholarship, the context (economic, social, and political) in which the parables came to be, and to see if Jesus used the parables to speak to that context. Granted, this requires imagination, with all the risks and the creative possibilities such imaginative interpretations present. I have concluded that the parables, as well as Jesus' whole life and death, make no sense if we don't account for the poverty of his peasant community life, and for the political oppression of the Roman occupation. Jesus' preaching and actions sought to heal both the physical and spiritual effects of that domination by an alien empire. This conclusion opens the parables so that they speak to the issues of poverty and oppression in all times – especially our own.

The second step has been the creation of sculptural images. This has allowed us to move beyond a verbal, discursive, and conceptual understanding of the parables, to an imaginative, intuitive and visual one, so that they may teach and guide us in a visionary way towards God's Empire and away from the empires of violence and fear.

Having made these images, I will now always think of the prodigal son returning to the overwhelming embrace of his father, and about the strangeness of his mother's absence. The friend at midnight will endure in my mind as a reminder of the importance of meeting the needs of the community, even when doing so may be annoying or inconvenient for me. The Samaritan image will press me to look at my "enemies" as those whose help I may need, and will make me wonder why the authorities protect some places and not others. The barren fig tree images will challenge me to find the courage to try to stop the slaughter of innocents. The image of the corrupt judge will remind me to be aware of the duplicity often found among authorities, and of the determination of the widow to expose such corruption and to find justice. The great supper images will stay in my mind as a welcome to *all* to feast with the divine. The fishnet, and wheat and tares images will relieve me of the temptation to judge others as being either evil or good, since "judging" is something best left to the Holy One. The two builders parable will insist that I walk the walk, that my deeds match my words. When I despair because of all the injustice, personal shame, and war in this world, I will remember the seed parables in Mark and know that God will bring a harvest of justice, honour, and peace. When I am heavy with guilt for deeds done and not done, I will think of the two debtors parable, and of the forgiven woman at Jesus' feet, who loved more because she had been forgiven more. Finally, the images of the hidden treasure and of the pearl merchant will move my feet to dance over the greatest of all treasures – God's Empire of justice, abundance, peace, hope, and courage.

Even though the empire of Rome has long since disappeared, fear, hate, and violence remain daily temptations and rule many parts of the world. This is because they gratify us immediately, while love requires determination and grit and the blessing of a God who promises courage when we need it most. My hope is that you will find as much wisdom in the parables, and in these images, as I have.

Bibliography of Consulted Sources

Adams, Doug. "Changing Perceptions of Jesus' Parables through Art History: Polyvalency in Paint." *Reluctant Partners: Art and Religion in Dialogue.* Ena Giurescu Heller, ed. New York: The Gallery of the American Bible Society, 2004. (Now the Museum of Biblical Art)

Apostolos-Cappadona, Dianne, ed. *Art, Creativity, and the Sacred: An Anthology in Religion and Art.* New York: Continuum, 1998.

Bailey, E. Kenneth. *Poet and Peasant and through Peasant Eyes: A Literary-Cultural Approach to the Parables of Luke* (Combined Edition). Grand Rapids: Wm. B. Eerdmans, 2000.

Beavis, Mary Ann, ed. *The Lost Coin: Parables of Women, Work and Wisdom.* New York: Sheffield Academic Press, a Continuum imprint, 2002.

Belting, Hans. *Likeness and Presence: A History of the Image before the Era of Art.* Edmund Jephcott, trans. Chicago: University of Chicago Press, 1996.

Bornkamm, Guenther. *Jesus of Nazareth.* Irene and Fraser McLuskey with James M. Robinson, trans. New York: Harper and Row, 1960.

Brown, Frank Burch. *Good Taste, Bad Taste, and Christian Taste: Aesthetics in Religious Life.* New York: Oxford University Press, 2000.

Bultmann, Rudolf. *History of the Synoptic Tradition.* John Marsh, trans. New York: Harper and Row, 1963.

— . *Jesus and the Word.* Louise Pettibone Smith and Erminie Huntress Lantero, trans. New York: Charles Scribner's Sons, 1958.

— . *Theology of the New Testament.* Vols. 1 and 2. Kendrick Goebel, trans. New York: Scribner's Sons. Volume 1. 1951. Volume 2. 1955.

— . and Karl Kundsin. *Form Criticism: Two Essays on New Testament Research.* Frederick C. Grant, trans. New York: Harper and Row, 1962.

Buttrick, David. *Speaking Parables: A Homiletic Guide.* Louisville: Westminster/John Knox Press, 2000.

Cadoux, A. T. *The Parables of Jesus: Their Art and Use.* New York: MacMillan Co., 1931.

Camara, Dom Helder. *Spiral of Violence.* London: Sheed and Ward, 1971.

Crossan, John Dominic. *Finding Is the First Act: Trove Folktales and Jesus' Treasure Parable.* Philadelphia: Fortress Press, 1979.

— . *In Parables: The Challenge of the Historical Jesus.* San Francisco: Harper and Row, 1973.

— . *Jesus: A Revolutionary Biography.* San Francisco: HarperSanFrancisco, 1994.

— . *The Essential Jesus: What Jesus Really Taught.* San Francisco: HarperSanFrancisco, 1995

— . *The Historical Jesus: The Life of a Mediterranean Jewish Peasant.* San Francisco: HarperSanFrancisco, 1992.

— . and Jonathan L. Reed. *In Search of Paul: How Jesus' Apostle Opposed Rome's Empire with God's Kingdom.* San Francisco: HarperSanFrancisco, 2004.

de Gruchy, John W. *Christianity, Art and Transformation: Theological Aesthetics in the Struggle for Justice.* Cambridge, UK: Cambridge University Press, 2001.

Dillenberger, Jane. *Image and Spirit in Secular and Sacred Art.* New York: Crossroad, 1990.

— . *Secular Art and Sacred Themes.* Nashville: Abingdon Press, 1969.

Dillenberger, John. *A Theology of Artistic Sensibilities: Visual Arts and the Church.* New York: Crossroad, 1986.

— . *Images and Relics: Theological Perceptions and Visual Images in Sixteenth-Century Europe.* Oxford, UK: Oxford University Press, 1999.

— . *The Visual Arts and Christianity in America.* New York: Crossroad, 1989.

Dodd, C. H. *The Parables of the Kingdom.* New York: Scribner and Sons, 1961.

Donahue, John R. *The Gospel in Parable.* Philadelphia: Fortress, 1988.

Drury, John. *Painting the Word: Christian Pictures and Their Meanings.* London: Yale University Press and National Gallery Publications, Limited, 1999.

— . *The Parables in the Gospels: History and Allegory.* London: SPCK, 1985.

Ehrman, Bart D. *Misquoting Jesus: The Story Behind Who Changed the Bible and Why.* San Francisco: HarperSanFrancisco, 2005.

Freier, Paulo. *Pedagogy of the Oppressed.* Myra Bergman Ramos, trans. New York: The Seabury Press, 1973.

Fuchs, Ernst. *Studies of the Historical Jesus.* Andrew Scobie, trans. Naperville, IL: Alec R. Allenson Inc.,1960.

Funk, Robert. *Honest to Jesus: Jesus for a New Millennium.* San Francisco: HarperSanFrancisco, 1996.

— . *Language, Hermeneutic, and Word of God.* New York: Harper and Row, 1966.

— . *Parables and Presence: Forms of the New Testament Tradition.* Philadelphia: Fortress, 1982.

— . et al. *The Five Gospels: The Search for the Authentic Words of Jesus.* New York: Macmillan, 1993.

— . et al. *The Parables of Jesus: Red Letter Edition.* Sonoma, California: Polebridge Press, 1988.

Hedrick, Charles W. *Parables as Poetic Fictions: The Creative Voice of Jesus.* Peabody, MA: Hendrickson Publishers, 1994.

Herzog, William R., II. *Parables as Subversive Speech: Jesus as Pedagogue of the Oppressed.* Louisville: Westminster/John Knox Press, 1994.

— . *Prophet and Teacher: An Introduction to the Historical Jesus.* Louisville: Westminster/John Knox Press, 2005.

Horsley, Richard A. *Jesus and Empire: The Kingdom of God and the New World Order.* Minneapolis: Fortress Press, 2003.

— . *Jesus and the Spiral of Violence: Popular Jewish Resistance in Roman Palestine.* San Francisco: Harper and Row, 1987.

Hultgren, Arland J. *The Parables of Jesus: A Commentary.* Grand Rapids: William B. Eerdmans Publishing Co., 2000.

Hunter, Archibald M. *Interpreting the Parables.* Philadelphia: Westminster Press, 1960.

Jeremias, Joachim. *The Parables of Jesus.* S. H. Hooke, trans. London: SCM Press, 1958.

Jones, Geraint Vaughan. *The Art and Truth of the Parables: A Study in their Literary Form and Modern Interpretation.* London: SPCK, 1964.

Jülicher, Adolf. *Die Gleichnisreden Jesu. 2 vols.* Tübingen: Mohr (Siebeck), 1910.

McCollough, Charles. *Faith Made Visible.* Cleveland: United Church Press, 2000.

— . *Resolving Conflict with Justice and Peace.* Cleveland: The Pilgrim Press, 1991.

McFague, Sally. *Speaking in Parables: A Study in Metaphor and Theology.* London: SCM Press, 2002.

— . *Super, Natural Christians: How We Should Love Nature.* Minneapolis: Fortress, 1997.

Myers, Ched. *Who Will Roll Away the Stone? Discipleship Queries for First World Christians.* Maryknoll, NY: Orbis Books, 2001.

Neyrey, Jerome H., ed. *The Social World of Luke-Acts: Models of Interpretation.* Peabody, Massachusetts: Hendrickson Publishers, 1991.

Patterson, Stephen J. *Beyond the Passion: Rethinking the Death and Life of Jesus.* Minneapolis: Fortress Press, 2004.

— . *The God of Jesus: The Historical Jesus and the Search for Meaning.* Harrisburg, PA: Trinity Press International, 1989.

Perrin, Norman. *Jesus and the Language of the Kingdom: Symbol and Metaphor in New Testament Interpretation.* Philadelphia: Fortress Press, 1974.

Reid, Barbara. *Parables for Preachers: The Gospel of Mark, Year B.* Collegeville, MN: The Liturgical Press, 1999.

— . *The Gospel of Luke, Year C.* Collegeville, MN: The Liturgical Press, 2000.

— . *The Gospel of Matthew, Year A.* Collegeville, MN: Liturgical Press, 2001.

Ringe, Sharon H. *Jesus, Liberation, and the Biblical Jubilee: Images for Ethics and Christology.* Philadelphia: Fortress, 1985.

Robinson, James M. and John B. Cobb, eds. *The New Hermeneutic: A Discussion among Continental and American Theologians.* Vol. II. New York: Harper and Row, 1964.

Schottroff, Luise. *The Parables of Jesus.* Linda M. Maloney, trans. Minneapolis: Fortress Press, 2006.

— . and Dorothee Soelle. *Jesus of Nazareth.* John Bowdon, trans. Louisville: Westminster/John Knox, 2002.

Scott, Bernard Brandon. *Hear Then the Parables: A Commentary on the Parables of Jesus.* Minneapolis: Fortress, 1989.

Via, Dan Otto. *The Parables: Their Literary and Existential Dimension.* Philadelphia: Fortress Press, 1967.

Vrudny, Kimberly and Wilson Yates, eds. *Arts, Theology, and the Church: New Intersections.* Cleveland: The Pilgrim Press, 2005.

Wilder, Amos N. *Jesus' Parables and the War of Myths: Essays on Imagination in the Scriptures.* Philadelphia: Fortress Press, 1982.

— . *New Testament Faith for Today.* New York: Harper and Row, 1955.

Wilson, A. N. *Paul: The Mind of the Apostle.* New York: W. W. Norton and Company, 1997.

Wink, Walter. *The Powers That Be: Theology for a New Millennium.* New York: Galilee/ Doubleday, 1998.

Wright, N. T. "Paul's Gospel and Caesar's Empire." *Reflections.* Vol. 2. (Spring 1999). Center of Theological Inquiry, Princeton, New Jersey.

Appendix - Parable Names and Parallels

	Luke	Mark	Matthew	Thomas	Other Names
1. Barren Fig Tree	13:1–9				Barren Tree
2. Children in the Market	7:18–35				Children in the Marketplace
3. Two Debtors	7:36–50				
4. Samaritan	10:25–37				Good Samaritan
5. Friend at Midnight	11:1–13				Importuned Friend
6. Rich Farmer	12:14–21			63	Rich Fool
7. Doorkeepers and Overseer	12:35–48	13:33–37	24:45–51		Returning Master
8. Great Supper	14:16–24		22:1–13	64	Great Feast, Feast
9. Tower and Warring King	14:25–33				
10. Lost Coin (and Sheep)	15:1–10		18:12–14	107	Lost Drachma
11. Prodigal and Elder Sons	15:11–32				Prodigal Son
12. Dishonest Manager	16:1–13				Unjust Steward
13. Rich Man and Lazarus	16:19–31				Lazarus and Dives
14. Corrupt Judge	18:1–8				Persistent Widow
15. Pharisee/Tax Collector	18:9–14				Pharisee and Publican
16. Sower	8:4–8	4:3–20	13:3–23	9	Types of Soil
17. Seed and Harvest		4:26–29		21	Seed Growing Secretly
18. Mustard Seed	13:18–19	4:31–32	13:31–32	20	
19. Absentee Landlord	20:9–18	12:1–12	21:33–34	65	Wicked Tenants
20 Two Builders	6:47–49		7:21–27		House Builders
21. Wheat and Tares			13:24–30	57	Planted Weeds
22. Leaven	13:20–21		13:33	96	Leaven in the Loaf
23. Treasure/Pearl Merchant			13:44–46	109, 76	Hidden Treasure/ Pearl of Great Price
24. Fishnet			13:47–50		Dragnet
25. Unforgiving Servant			18:21–35		Unmerciful Servant
26. Vineyard Workers	20:9–18	12:1–12	20:1–16		Labourers in the Vineyard
37. Two Children			21:28–32		Two Sons
28. Young Women	13:25		25:1–13		Ten Virgins, Closed Door
29. Talents	19:11–21		25:14–30		Entrusted Money
30. Last Judgement			25:31–46		

Note: These are the most frequently used names, but there are many other names given to the parables. Also note that the pairs of parables (The Lost Coin and The Lost Sheep, The Tower and The Warring King, and The Treasure and The Pearl Merchant) are separate parables but are analyzed together following their paired locations in the gospels.

After completing his Ph.D. in Theology, CHARLES McCOLLOUGH worked for the national staff of the United Church of Christ in the areas of adult education and social justice. At the same time, he pursued his love of art, studying sculpture at the Pennsylvania Academy of Fine Arts, Johnson Atelier, the Princeton Art Association, and Mercer College. He has taught art and social ethics, sculpted, and lectured on themes such as human rights, peace and justice. He is the author of six previous books: *Morality of Power, Heads of Heaven/ Feet of Clay, Lifestyles of Faithfulness, To Love the Earth, Resolving Conflict with Justice* and *Peace, and Faith Made Visible.*